M000289881

A NEW ORCHARD AND GARDEN
with
THE COUNTRY HOUSEWIFES GARDEN

A NEW ORCHARD AND GARDEN

WITH

THE COUNTRY HOUSEWIFES GARDEN

WILLIAM LAWSON

A FACSIMILE EDITION
WITH AN INTRODUCTION
BY

MALCOLM THICK

PROSPECT BOOKS

2003

This edition first published in Great Britain in 2003 by Prospect Books, Allaleigh House, Blackawton, Totnes, Devon TQ9 7DL.

© 2003, Prospect Books.
© 2003, for the introduction, Malcolm Thick.

The first edition of *A New Orchard and Garden* and *The Country Housewifes Garden* was published in 1618. This facsimile is taken from the printing of 1656 in Gervase Markham's *A Way to get Wealth*, itself first published in 1623. Prospect Books is grateful to Malcolm Thick for the loan of the book.

A CIP record for this book is available from the British Library.

ISBN 1-903018-10-2

Designed and typeset by Tom Jaine.

Printed and bound in Great Britain by the Cromwell Press, Trowbridge, Wiltshire.

CONTENTS

INTRODUCTION

A New Orchard and Garden and *The Country Housewifes Garden* were first published together in 1618, despite the date of 1617 on the title-page of *The Country Housewifes Garden*. Subsequent joint publications appeared in 1623 and 1626: the books were also absorbed into a collection of works on cookery, agriculture and gardening by Gervase Markham entitled *A Way to get Wealth,* which was published about fifteen times between 1623 and 1695. Lawson's works were, therefore, some of the best-known books on orchards and gardens in the seventeenth century.[1]

A resurgence of interest in Lawson in the twentieth century, principally because of his book for women gardeners, saw several new editions. In 1926 Cresset Press produced an edition in an elegant type with an introduction by the most prominent garden historian of the day, Eleanor Sinclair Rohde. A private-press edition in 1948 was followed by the publication of *The Country Housewifes Garden* together with extracts from *A New Orchard and Garden* in 1983, with an introduction from another renowned writer on gardening, Rosemary Verey. In America, Lawson was republished in Philadelphia in 1858 and, in the last century, the books appeared in 1940 and 1982.[2]

In view of this extensive publishing history, why do we need another edition? None of the previous publications is in print and

[1] Blanche Henrey, *British Botanical and Horticultural Literature before 1800,* 1975, vol. I, pp. 158–60; F.N.L. Pointer, *A Bibliography of Gervase Markham,* Oxford Bibliographical Society, 1962, pp. 152–178.
[2] See *Library of Congress* catalogue at *www.loc.gov.catalog/* for details of the American editions.

old copies are difficult, and expensive, to obtain. This present edition will be the first facsimile for some time, preserving both the layout and typography, and the illustrations. In past introductions much has been made of William Lawson's prose and his advice on gardening and garden design. Whilst covering these topics myself, I wish also to produce a portrait of William Lawson, his philosophy and outlook on the world as well as the known details of his life, discuss the reasons for his producing the books, and look at how Lawson's work was perceived later in the seventeenth century.

The two books were published together and meant so to be – frequent mention is made of *A New Orchard* in *The Country House-wifes Garden* and some very short chapters in the second are little more than a couple of sentences referring the reader back to the former book. The books are, however, different in style. *A New Orchard* proceeds at a more leisurely pace, with chapters largely devoted to the philosophy of gardening and the pleasures and profits to be derived from a well-stocked orchard. Latin quotations, proverbs, classical allusions are scattered through *A New Orchard* but are not found in *The Country Housewifes Garden* which is, for the most part, a sparely written manual. Only when talking of flowers and bees does Lawson allow himself to be diverted from the task of giving housewives clear and simple instructions.

The illustrations in both books have been frequently reproduced, and deservedly so: Lawson insisted that the publisher expended 'much cost and care … in having the Knots & Models by the best Artizan cut in great variety'. The half-page woodcut of gardeners digging, and cutting and planting slips is a delight to the eye: no wonder the printer used it both in the text and as a frontispiece. *The perfect form of a Fruit-tree* on page 36 [70] is at the same time a simple diagram and a bold and lively design. Lawson's idea of an ideal orchard and garden on page 10 [44] is another example of a bold but pleasing plan, enlivened with suggested topiary figures, a knot, and an old-fashioned fountain. (A very similar fountain occupies the centre of a garden in Markham's *English Husbandman*.)

The knot in this garden is not typical. The plates of suggested knots included in this book are based on a square plot subdivided by a grid and diagonals (see page 71 [95]), as are all knots found in other sixteenth-century and early seventeenth-century gardening books. One cannot produce the knot on page 10 [44], a six-pointed star surrounding a double five-petalled rose, using a squared base. The design, including a small 'c' in the centre of the rose, would not look out of place in a Rosicrucian emblem book, but we cannot ascribe to a Yorkshire vicar such outlandish ideas.

✳ ✳ ✳

Until the 1980s all that was known about William Lawson came from these two small books: his great age and long experience in gardening; that he lived for a long time in Yorkshire; was well-versed in the Bible, the classics and some Continental books of natural history; was acquainted with 'that honourable Lady at Hackness' Lady Margaret Hoby; and had seen a stranded whale at Teesmouth and a blown-down pear tree at Wilton in Cleveland.

In 1982 John Harvey, correctly guessing that Lawson was a clergyman, identified him as the vicar of Ormesby, a Yorkshire parish at Teesmouth, from 1583 until his death, aged 82, in 1635. He was twice married and spent the whole of his career in the north of England. His son, another William, also joined the church, in 1622 becoming vicar of Stainton, only three miles from his father's parish. His landholding consisted of a considerable part of the parish of Ormesby and John Harvey speculated[3] that the ideal garden set out in *A New Orchard* may have been based on an idea for land held by Lawson at the mouth of the Tees. He was, for a country vicar, a man

[3] John Harvey, 'William Lawson and his Orchard', *Country Life*, Oct. 28, 1982, pp. 1338–40.

of some learning. The two books he published have references to classical authors, as well as to Erasmus and to a work on the West Indies by Peter Martyr. He was also acquainted with English works on agriculture and gardening. He had a library of books, probably works on religion and philosophy, and when he died willed 'all mie latine books & mie English books of contraversie' to his son William.[4]

He ministered during a time when the Church of England was still a relatively young institution with great doctrinal struggles taking place within it. He had at least one friend known for her Protestant piety, Lady Margaret Hoby, and his religious convictions were broadly puritan – he had no truck with 'popery and knavery'.[5] A vicar of long standing, he understood the weaknesses of those to whom he ministered and the need for firm moral guidance. 'Man himself left to himself, growes from his heavenly and spirituall generation, and becometh beastly, yea, devilish to his own kind, unlesse he be regenerate.' He took his calling seriously and was described in ecclesiastical records as *Pastor vigilantissimus* and *catechista diligentissimus*, a most diligent teacher and vigilant priest. He built the pulpit in his own church and it is sobering to reflect that, whilst we remember him for his gardening books, he was most proud of his preaching. In his will (which he wrote himself) he directs that he be buried under or near the pulpit at Ormesby. On his tombstone he wished a Latin epitaph to be inscribed which freely translates as:

> This pulpit's donor adorned it for so long as he taught
> the people God's Holy Writ from it. Scorning worldly
> protectresses and loves, he has lain down under the
> pulpit where once he stood. In the grave, the soul,

[4] Will of William Lawson, 10 September 1635, Chancery. *Borthwick Institute*, York.
[5] Harvey, op. cit., p. 1340. In the preamble of his will Lawson is sure he has been saved 'through Christ', implying a belief in the Puritan doctrine of election.

trusting to the last in the pulpit, climbs Olympus,
while the flesh, turned to ashes, remains.[6]

Indeed, parts of the chapter on the age of trees read like extracts
from one of his sermons: 'Physic holds it possible, that a clean body
kept by these three Doctors, *Doctor Diet, Doctor Quiet,* and *Doctor
Merryman,* may live neer a hundred years.' Methuselah lived long
but men say that life became shorter after the Flood; men, he wrote,
have shortened their lives by 'want of knowledge, evill Government,
Riot, Gluttony, Drunkennesse, and (to be short) the encrease of the
curse, our sins increasing in an Iron and wicked age.' If men 'whose
course of life cannot by any means, by Counsell, restraint of Lawes
or punishment, nor hope of praise, profit, or eternall glory, be kept
within bounds', can live to a hundred, is it any wonder that well-
tended trees can live so much longer?

One can imagine Lawson urging his congregation to live clean,
quiet, sober lives like trees!

Although he took his calling seriously, Lawson was much more
than a stern moralist. The delight in trees, flowers, herbs, bees, birds
and all of nature which shines through his books leave one with the
impression of a kindly man, content with life. He could crack a joke
– country housewives who found any of his rules for gardening
'knotty' were referred to chapter 3 (the chapter on garden knots). He
liked music and singing, enjoying the sound of the organ and 'a sweet
Recorder'. His ideal garden would have space for 'silver sounding

---

[6] I am very grateful to Jim McMahon for deciphering the original Latin poem from
an indistinct manuscript and translating it into English. The original epitaph is:
'Qui tibi rostra dedit stans rostra decorat
Dum populum docuit dogmata sacra die.
Postquam fautrices mundi contempsit amores,
Succubuit rostris, in quibus ille stetit.
Spiritus rostro serum fidens conscendit olimpum
In tumulo, in cineres, dum caro versa manet.'

Musicke, mixt instruments, and voyces'. He bequeathed to his grandson 'all mie song books' and one can imagine the Lawson family in consort singing and playing under his trees of a summer evening. His strict morality was tempered by a keen sense of social justice. Giving away surplus fruit to neighbours would discourage pilfering, 'For as liberality will save it best from noisome neighbours, (Liberality I say is the best fence) so justice must restrain Rioters.' He uses such phrases twice in the book. The mention of rioters may be a reference to disturbances in the 1590s when near-famine conditions in parts of England followed harvest failures and the governing classes had to tread a fine line between condemning the disturbances and urging that the poor be sold food at reasonable rates.

❋ ❋ ❋

The title-page, preface and dedication of *A New Orchard* tell us for whom the books were written and Lawson's reasons for producing them. *A New Orchard* is to impart the best way to run an orchard 'particularly in the North'. Several times in the book Lawson highlights the climatic constraints of the north of England – shorter summers, harsher winters, deep snow, etc. Lawson had read many of the existing books on gardening and orchards, finding them written by men from the south or, even worse, translated from classical writers whose instruction was more suited to the shores of the Mediterranean.[7] He acknowledged the insight of classical authors but proposed to 'leave them to their times, manners, and several Countries'. He was at pains to assure his readers that his books were original, written 'of my meere and sole Experience', the wisdom of an old man 'All being the experience of Forty and eight

---

[7] Gervase Markham wrote in similar vein in his introduction to *The English Husbandman*, first published in 1613 (which Lawson may well have read), complaining of translations of classical and foreign works by men who were 'all Forrainers and utterly unacquainted with our Climes.'

yeares labour'. 'Art,' he explained, 'hath her first originall out of Experience ... therefore must we count that art the surest, that stands upon Experimentall Rules, gathered by the rule of Reason'.

The dedication is to Sir Henry Belloses (Belasyse), a prominent Yorkshire baronet with a house at Newburgh who was 'renowned for his hospitality'.[8] Like Lawson, he was keenly interested in orchards, helping him and others with 'learned Discourses of Fruit-trees'. Lawson may have given advice in return: Sir Roy Strong has noted a similarity between the knot at the bottom of page 73 [97] ('Lozenges') and part of the garden at Sir Henry's seat, Newburgh Priory, as depicted in a painting of the late seventeenth century. Lady Margaret Hoby, who lived at Hackness about thirty miles from Lawson, was another member of the local gentry named by him as interested in gardening. One has the impression that Lawson was part of a thriving group of gentry-gardeners in Yorkshire, some of whom had persuaded him to publish his works, they having admired his gardens when they 'resorted to me to confer in matters of that nature'.[9]

Lawson opens *A New Orchard* with a chapter defining in detail the qualities of a good employed gardener, a topic not previously tackled by gardening writers. As a cleric of some piety, Lawson begins by saying a gardener should be religious in both thought and deed, specifying quite closely the orthodoxy to which he should aspire. A gardener was one of the most important servants in a household and should set an example to the others, upholding the good name of the family and helping 'to stay unbridled Serving men' who might listen to evil counsel. He had to be honest and hard working, keeping to his tasks throughout the year, but not doing untold harm by carrying out jobs at which he had no skill. The master had an obligation to allow the gardener help in summer to

[8] G.E. Cokayne, *Complete Baronetage*, 1900, vol. I, p. 43.
[9] Sir Roy Strong, *The Artist and the Garden*, 2000, pp. 152–3.

harvest the fruit and he should augment the gardener's wages, after the house was well served, with 'fallen fruit, superfluity of hearbs, and flowers, seeds, graffes, Sets'. If one employed such a paragon, the whole task of gardening could be left to him and gentlemen and women could ignore a book like Lawson's! Recollecting this, he adds a final paragraph recommending what follows to those 'not able, nor willing to hire a Gardener'.

The remaining chapters of *A New Orchard* can be divided between those primarily giving instruction and advice, and reflective or philosophical passages in which Lawson expatiates on the profits, pleasures, comfort and spiritual renewal to be gained from orchards and gardens, giving his views on garden design and incidentally telling us something of his own garden and his outlook on life. We will look first at the instructional parts of *A New Orchard* which cover all aspects of orchard-keeping, from the choice and preparation of the ground, to gathering and storing of fruit from mature trees.

Lawson's advice is practical and sensible. In discussing the tilth he suggests good soil, a level, moist site, and cautions against excessive digging which might disturb the topsoil. A low-lying site near a river is the best,[10] for here good soil washed down from hills will have accumulated and there will be some shelter from harsh weather. He stresses this opinion with examples of low-lying, riparian sites in Yorkshire and abroad, 'I have stood somewhat long in this poynt, because some do condemn a moist soyl for fruit trees'.[11] He is content to confine his orchard to the fruit which can

---

[10] Was he here influenced by the site of his own orchard?

[11] A sidenote refers to *Mr Markham* who, in *The English Husbandman,* p. 126 (1635 edition), advises against moist ground near rivers for orchards. Lawson makes several cross-references to this book, which first appeared four years before his own and was also based on observation rather than a translation. Markham's section on orchards is detailed and, whilst not agreeing with all he wrote, Lawson seems to have regarded this work as the best publication he had seen and a yardstick against which to judge his own work.

withstand 'these frozen parts', spending some time decrying attempts to grow cherries, apricots and peaches as wall fruit because the unnatural training of trees against walls does great damage and they die ten times sooner than free-growing trees.

Lawson was keen to encourage men to plant large orchards but he saw difficulties if the land was not held on a secure tenure. He suggested longer leases be granted to take account of the time taken for an orchard to become profitable. Influenced perhaps by James I's scheme for mulberry trees to feed silk worms, he also suggests legislation forcing landholders to plant so many acres of fruit trees of a specified type.

Chapters on fences and 'Annoyances' advise how to keep out animals and thieves and protect trees against disease, weather, and attacks by deer, moles ('moles will anger you' he says candidly), hares, birds and other pests. A moat and broad bank set with quicksets is his preferred option for fencing.

The chapters on raising sets, planting an orchard, manuring, grafting and pruning are the most technical parts of the book, drawing on his own skill and what he himself learned from books and other orchard-keepers. English gardeners had long been interested in fruit growing, and the first manual on the care of fruit trees was published in the 1520s.[12] These chapters are those which would have been examined most critically by his own circle of orchard lovers and they were re-examined later in the century by writers, working first under the Commonwealth and then with the Royal Society, who were collecting together useful information on agriculture, horticulture and manufacturing to encourage enterprise in the Kingdom.

John Beale, another fruit-growing clergyman who became a Fellow of the Royal Society in January 1663, wrote two letters to Samuel Hartlib, the leading promoter of agricultural improvement

[12] Henrey, vol. I, p. 57.

of his day, which were subsequently published as *Herefordshire orchards, a pattern for all England* in 1657. Beale cites a number of authors in this pamphlet but none is examined in such depth as William Lawson. Beale tells us that,

> Some Years ago I read a small Treatise of Orchards and Gardens by William Lawson, a North-Country Man, Printed 1626. In it I found many assertions which seemed to me so strange, so contrary to our general Opinion, so discordant from our daily Practice, and so incredible, that I could not forbear my smiles. I related the particulars to all our best Artists. Every Man confirmed me, that the Treatise was wholly ridiculous, and in no respect worthy to be examined and weighed: yet I thought I found many signs of Honesty and Integrity in the Man, a sound, clear, natural wit, and all things attested and affirm'd upon his own Experiences. This raised my Wonder the more.[13]

Despite this discouragement, Beale subjected five of Lawson's opinions about growing apples to 'exact trial with patience' and found that much of what he wrote was true.

John Evelyn, another Royal Society member, compiled *Sylva,* an imposing book on forest and fruit trees, at the behest of the Society in 1664. The book aimed to bring together the best writing on trees to encourage gentlemen to plant trees both for timber and fruit – particularly cider apples. Much of Evelyn's chapter on pruning is taken from Lawson. Following initial remarks on pruning, Evelyn introduces one and a half pages of direct quotation from Lawson (and several further pages of summary) thus:

[13] J[ohn] B[eale], *Hertfordshire orchards, a pattern for all England*, 2nd ed., 1724, pp. 8–9.

Divers other precepts of this nature I could here enumerate, had not the great *experience*, faithful, and accurate *description* how this necessary work is to be perform'd, set down by our Country-man honest *Lawson (Orchard, cap. 11)* prevented all that the most *Inquisitive* can suggest: The particulars are so ingenious, and highly material, that you will not be displeas'd to read them in his own style.

Evelyn also repeated with approval Lawson's extensive remarks on the age of trees (one of the topics also discussed by Beale), concluding that 'The Discourse is both learned, rational, and full of encouragement', and describing Lawson as 'Our honest Countryman, to whose Experience we have been obliged.' *A New Orchard* was, it appears, in the mid-seventeenth century, regarded as a standard text on trees.[14]

Lawson's instructions on gathering fruit are succinct: stand upon a ladder with 'A gathering-apron like a poak before you, made of purpose, or a wallet hung on a bough, or a basket with a sieve bottome, or skin bottome, with lathes or splinters under, hung in a rope to pull up and down.' Gathered fruit was to be first dried, then, in a dry loft, 'lay them thin abroad'. Fruit kept successfully for much of the year was a great boon to a household, adding variety, freshness and sweetness to a diet often of necessity dull and bland. The purpose-made baskets and 'poaks' he mentions are just some of the many instruments, a few of which are illustrated, which Lawson recommends for maintaining an orchard.

❉ ❉ ❉

Three chapters of *A New Orchard* – on profits, the age of trees, and ornaments – are reflective and philosophical rather than instructional.

[14] John Evelyn, *Sylva*, 1670, pp. 143, 148.

The short chapter on profits, at the end of those describing the making and maintaining of orchards, begins, 'Now pause with yourselfe, and view the end of all your Labours in an Orchard: unspeakable pleasure, and infinite commodity.' This combination of profit and pleasure, reiterated in the following chapter, is a constant theme in seventeenth-century horticultural literature (and, according to Markham, is found in earlier Continental books),[15] particularly with regard to orchards where, unlike purely ornamental gardens, any guilt at creating something for enjoyment can be assuaged by the profit of the fruit and other produce grown. Another 'godly' man, Ralph Austen, had this conjunction vividly depicted on the title-page of his book on orchards in 1553: two strong arms emerge from clouds labelled 'Profits' and 'Pleasures' and clasp hands firmly.[16]

Lawson maintains that half an acre of Orchard is more profitable than one acre of corn, and that orchards are more profitable than gardens. Such profitability was a frequent theme of writers a generation later – Walter Blith in the 1650s maintained that orchards planted on relatively poor land could increase the rent twentyfold, and Ralph Austen took it as 'very well known to many in this Nation' that orchards were very profitable.[17] By the middle of the century, writers could draw on the example of actual commercial orchards for these claims.[18] Lawson lists profitable produce: cider and perry, for which he gives a simple recipe; raw fruit for home consumption or sale; distilled waters from the flowers and herbs in the orchard (roses, woodbine or angelica); and profits from crops grown between the trees such as saffron or liquorice. A wide variety of crops could be grown, he wrote, between young trees in the years

---

[15] Markham, *English Husbandman*, 1635, p. 119.
[16] Ralph Austen, *A treatise of fruit trees*, Oxford, 1653.
[17] Austen, op. cit., p. 1; Walter Blith, *The English Improver Improved*, 1653, p. 267.
[18] Samuel Hartlib, *Legacy of Husbandry*, 1655, p. 15.

before their maturity. Growing crops between trees was popular at the end of the nineteenth century in England when it was known as 'the Kent system'. Joan Thirsk describes how, 'Rows of fruit trees in orchards were separated by rows of vegetables, so that no land was left idle which could accommodate a crop. At Evesham, for example, Rider Haggard described broad beans, lettuces, parsley, potatoes, cabbages, and radishes growing between fruit trees. At Ledbury, Herefordshire, soft fruits were grown between standard fruit trees on a farm of 40 acres.'[19]

Lawson's chapter on the age of trees is a digression which allows him to bring together evidence from the Bible, classical literature (Cicero, *De Senectute*, and Erasmus 'out of Hesiodus'), and to demonstrate his powers of argument, producing a case for the extreme longevity of trees. He takes the opportunity also to draw moral conclusions from the life-expectancy of trees.

The final chapter in *A New Orchard* considers 'Ornaments' and here Lawson describes, and justifies, the pleasure of an orchard adorned with borders of flowers and herbs and a number of other garden features. Work itself is a pleasure in an orchard and people should have no qualms about using an orchard for rest and recreation, for God placed Man in Paradise, 'And who can deny but the Principal end of an Orchard, is the honest delight of one wearied with the works of his lawfull calling?' Mindful perhaps of the gentry who were the likely readers of his book, Lawson flatteringly calls them 'the gods of the earth' who, wearied of the cares of the law and government (and stuffy buildings and fine banquets), go to their orchards 'to renew and refresh their senses, and call home their over-wearied spirits.'

Orchards please all the senses, 'What can your eye desire to see, your eares to heare, your mouth to taste, or your nose to smell, that is not to be had in an Orchard, with abundance of variety?' Lawson

[19] Joan Thirsk, *Alternative Agriculture*, 1997, p. 175.

was particularly fond of birds in an orchard (and forgave them the fruit they took): blackbirds, thrushes, robins, wrens, and especially nightingales 'who with several notes and tunes, with a strong and delightsome voyce out of a weak body, will beare you company night and day.'

Much of this chapter describes Lawson's ideal orchard and garden, adding to the outline in the illustration and side notes on page 10 [44]. John Harvey suggested that Lawson had a site in mind, by the mouth of the Tees, for this garden. His actual orchard was a more humble affair, 'my little Orchard' , the trees in which were at least forty years old when he first came to Ormesby.

This ideal garden is terraced, on three levels with steps between, with a moat separating it from the house in the south and a river (the Tees) flowing by to the north. Bounded on the east by a double plantation of woods to keep out the wind, the garden has six compartments for trees, knots, topiary work and kitchen gardens. Four mounts topped with two still-houses and two gazebos stand in the corners, with two sheltered spots for bee skeps by the river. Space might be found also for a bowling alley, archery butts, or a maze.

Miles Hadfield thought Lawson's directions for laying out a garden 'not very helpful',[20] but they do typify the ideals of Tudor and Stuart gentry gardens. Such a garden would have been considered old-fashioned by the most fashion-conscious (and rich) gentlemen of the day who were already spending money on grander 'Renaissance' gardens influenced by Italy and in many cases laid out by Continental gardeners.[21] But the gardens favoured by Lawson and his friends 'had an intimacy never regained once the impact of the high Italian Renaissance and the French grand manner reached

---

[20] Miles Hadfield, *A History of British Gardening*, 1960, p. 76.
[21] For example, the gardens created at this time by Solomon de Caus for royal and aristocratic patrons.

England'.[22] Rather then describe the ideal garden in detail, I will leave the reader to imagine it from Lawson's prose and plan.

✳ ✳ ✳

The Country Housewifes Garden has some fame as the first gardening book for women, but present-day readers must not expect to see in it evidence of a change in the attitude of men to women. Lawson had respect for women, but treated them differently from men. No references to the classics and few Latin quotations are found in this book, no digressions on philosophy, morality or social justice. The text is for the most part plain, simple and didactic. It was assumed the housewife had little experience of books – a note on the title-page tells her how to find the contents-page. Lawson is at pains not to overload the housewife with too much information, describing only those vegetables, herbs and flowers necessary for starting a basic country garden 'because I teach my *Country Housewife*, not skilfull Artists'. Even though the garden was to be created by a woman, Lawson leaves the size of it to be decided by 'every mans ability and will'.

Why, then, was the book written? It was published not long after Sir Hugh Plat's *Delights for Ladies*, a book of food, medicines and cosmetics aimed specifically at women which in turn had been preceded by several cookery books for women. Gervase Markham wrote *The English Housewife* in 1615, a large book covering cookery, medicine, distilling, the dairy, baking, brewing and malting, clothmaking and dyeing. *The Country Housewifes Garden* was part of a general interest (on the part of men) in women's work. It has been suggested to me that the shock of bad harvests in the 1590s and the general strain on resources occasioned by rising population caused men to place more value on the contribution women could make to a household by gardening, beekeeping, dairying, distilling,

[22] J.S. Berrall, *The Garden*, 1978, p. 241.

weaving and spinning as well as producing food, drink, clothing and medicine, particularly in times of scarcity.[23]

Whatever the motivation, Lawson wrote a little book which is packed with interesting advice. It was written after *A New Orchard* and many chapters are very short, explaining that the advice on, say, fences or the site for a garden is similar to that for an orchard. Several pages of knots adorn the book although Lawson leaves 'every houswife to herself' to devise a suitable design. He does, however, go into some detail on the form of a simple country garden, advising two divisions, for flowers and for kitchen vegetables. Practical reasons for the distinction are that vegetables mature at different times, leaving some beds untidy or bare whereas in a formal garden the planting remains fixed for a season. Also, there was a constant need to get amongst the vegetables to weed and harvest them. Detailed and sensible directions on making narrow beds for vegetables to provide good access recall the little book by Richard Gardiner on kitchen gardening published a few years earlier.[24]

The longest chapter on gardening itself is the 'Husbandry of Herbs', an alphabetical list of vegetables, fruits, flowers and herbs for a country garden, each with advice on growing and their culinary or medicinal qualities. The individual entries are short and practical: when to plant seeds, which are renewed by root division, large vegetables which require a plot to themselves, etc. This is a very traditional way of introducing garden crops, a similar format to medieval plant-lists.[25] Lawson cannot resist putting some flowers of no practical use in the list – for example gilly-flowers whose utility is 'much in ornament, and comforting the spirits'.

---

[23] Joan Thirsk put this idea to me in a conversation. I hope I have reflected accurately her thoughts.

[24] Richard Gardiner, *Profitable instructions for the manuring, sowing, and planting of kitchin gardens*, 1599.

[25] See, for example, *Pietro Crescentio, Opera di Agricoltura*, Venice, 1534, written in the fourteenth century.

Two short chapters, essentially just lists and short apophthegms, typify Lawson's didactic approach. In the 'Division of Herbs' he simply groups crops for a country garden into three divisions according to their size. Chapter IX, 'General Rules in Gardening', reduces to sixteen rules all that a housewife needs to know to start a garden in the north of England, followed by a final extra tip – be present when your maids weed, or teach them well to distinguish between weeds and crops.

✳ ✳ ✳

Lawson concludes his advice to country housewives with a section on beekeeping. He, like Thomas Tusser before him and a succession of writers afterwards, assumed that countrywomen would be responsible for bees and honey. Although sugar was a more stylish sweetener, honey was cheaper and had many more domestic uses than to sweeten food. It was a soothing ingredient in medicine and a medium in which to take unpalatable prescriptions. It was known as a preservative. Drinks made from honey – mead, metheglin – were popular at the time: Sir Kenelm Digby collected a large number of recipes which were published in his 'Closet' in 1669, many from noblemen and women.[26]

Interest in bees in the sixteenth century was reflected in some translations of foreign works and classical texts and, in 1593, the first original English bee-book by Edmund Southerne. A major work, the Reverend Charles Butler's *The feminine monarchie*, appeared in 1609. Many clergymen, including Lawson, wrote on bees, maybe the apparently ordered lives of bees ('cleanly and innocent' he called them) provided consolation to a vicar trying to instil morality into sometimes difficult parishioners. Lawson found bees to 'love their

---

[26] Penelope Walker & Eva Crane, 'The history of beekeeping in English gardens', *Garden History*, vol. 28, 2, 2000, p. 234; *The Closet of Sir Kenelm Digby Opened*, ed. Jane Stevenson & Peter Davidson, Totnes, 1997.

friends, and hate none but their enemies'. They were trusting of those they knew, and paid for their keep 'with great profit' – altogether an ideal flock for a world-weary clergyman. Lawson acknowledges earlier writers on bees who have written in more detail, some 'well and truly', but being for many years a 'Bee-master' he has some original material to contribute.[27]

In 1614 Gervase Markham dealt with bees in the first edition of *Cheape and good husbandry* and Lawson refers to this work, disagreeing with Markham's preference for wooden hives. Despite the risk of invasion by mice, Lawson preferred straw skeps 'which I commend for nimblenesse, closenesse, warmnesse, and drynesse'. Lawson described and included an illustration of an open-sided wooden structure, set in the corner of a wall, in which to house the bees which was preferably to be sited in the orchard 'for bees love flowers and wood with their hearts'. In the opinion of modern bee-keepers 'a comparison between the bee matter in *Cheape and good husbandry* and Lawson's *A New Orchard and Garden* shows Lawson to be the better practical bee keeper.' His few pages on bees are full of useful advice, concluding with directions on extracting honey from combs and storing it.[28]

Lawson claimed that 'if you have but forty stocks' of bees they would yield 'more commodity clearly than forty Acres of Ground'. But, as with orchards, Lawson had a great affection for bees and one has a feeling that had they produced no useful honey or wax, he would still have recommended a hive or two in his orchard 'to sing, and sit, and feed upon your flowers and sprouts, make a pleasant noyse and sight.'

✳ ✳ ✳

[27] Edmund Southerne, *A treatise concerning the right ordering of bees*, 1593; Rev. Charles Butler, *The feminine monarchie*, 1609; J.P. Harding et al., *British Bee Books*, 1979, pp. 36–46.
[28] Harding et al., op. cit., pp. 36–46.

A short note on the little treatises at the end of the book.
Appended to the second edition of Lawson's book in 1623 and to
subsequent editions were two small works, *A Most Profitable new
treatise, from approved experience of the Art of Propagating Plants,* by
Simon Harward and *The Husband Mans Fruitful Orchard.* I can find
no information on Harward but his little treatise contains, within
its twelve pages, evidence of a wealth of knowledge about layering
and grafting trees covering all the main methods of the day.
Harward's attention to detail is evident before he starts to describe
grafting when he sets out all the equipment necessary, beginning:
'The furniture and tools of a Grafter, are a basket to lay his grafts
in, Clay, Gravell, Sand, or strong Earth to draw over the plants
cloven, Moss, Woollen cloaths, barks of Willow to joyn to the late
things and earth before spoken,' and continuing the list with osiers
for binding, gummed wax to cover grafts newly cut, a hand-saw, a
penknife, one broad and one thin wedge in a hard wood, and a little
hand-bill with an ivory or hard-wood handle.

The last page of this treatise, which is not mentioned in the
contents list, is a paragraph headed 'A very profitable Invention, for
the speedy Planting of an Orchard of Fruit-Trees'. The writing style
is not Harward's and this appears to be a stray piece of manuscript
which the publisher has added. It details the practice of air-layering,
producing roots in the branch of a tree by stripping the bark from
part of it and binding earth to it. Once roots have set, the limb is
cut off and planted to form a new tree.[29]

The Husband Mans Fruitful Orchard is an abbreviated version of
the anonymous *The Fruiterers Secrets* first published in 1604, with
a dedication and epistle signed 'N.F.'. The author claimed to be
'Irish-borne'. He dedicated the original work to a Lord Lieutenant
of Ireland, and in the epistle details the work of another Irishman,

---

[29] *The Royal Horticultural Society Encyclopedia of Gardening,* ed. Christopher
Brickell, 1992, p. 57.

Richard Harris, fruiterer to Henry VIII who brought over new varieties of fruit trees from France and the Low Countries to his orchard in Kent, greatly stimulating commercial fruit-growing there. This work, even in the truncated form published here, is a plainly-written and practical description of how to harvest and transport delicate fruit with as little damage as possible. Those in business as growers were the most likely to encounter transport problems and talk of carriage by horse-pannier and ship make it likely that the author was a commercial fruiterer from north Kent, experienced in the London trade. As anyone who has today brought a paper bag of cherries home from the market will appreciate, these fruit bruise with the slightest pressure.[30]

My final note regards the second of the two copies of Markham's *A Way to get Wealth* (containing the Lawson pamphlets) in my possession. (The facsimile has been derived from my other copy, a slightly earlier impression.) On the final page are some anonymous manuscript scribbles as well as some notes of account in a seventeenth-century hand. These relate to three payments towards the cost of nursing a child. Hardly proof positive, but they may go some way towards a conclusion that William Lawson's *Country Housewifes Garden* was indeed possessed by one woman at least.

Malcolm Thick,
Harwell, January 2003.

[30] Henrey, vol. I, pp. 156–7

A NEW ORCHARD AND GARDEN
with
THE COUNTRY HOUSEWIFES GARDEN

A new ORCHARD, and GARDEN:
OR,

The beſt way for Planting, Grafting, and to make any ground good, for a rich Orchard: Particularly in the North, and generally for the whole Common-wealth, as in nature, reaſon, ſituation, and all probability, may and doth appeare.

With the Country-houſwifes Garden for Herbs of Common uſe: their Virtues, Seaſons, Profits, Ornaments, variety of Knots, Models for Trees, and Plots, for the beſt ordering of Grounds and Walkes.

AS ALSO

The Husbandry of Bees, with their ſeverall Uſes and Annoyances
Allb ing the experience of Forty and eight yeares labour, and now the ſecond time corrected and much enlarged, by WILLIAM LAWSON.

Whereunto is newly added the Art of Propagating Plants; with the true ordering of all manner of Fruits, in their gathering; carrying home, and preſervation.

Skill and pains, bring fruitfull gains.

Nemo ſibi natus.

London, Printed by *W. Wilſon*, for *E. Brewſter*, and *George Sawbridge*, at the Bible on Ludgate-Hill, neere *Fleet-bridge*. 1656.

To the Right Worshipfull
Sir HENRY BELLOSES,
Knight and *Baronet.*

Worthy Sir,

Hen in many years by long experience I had furnished this my Northerne Orchard and Country Garden with needfull Plants and usefull *Hearbes,* I did impart the view thereof to my Friends, who resorted to me to confer in matters of that nature; they did see it, and seeing it, desired it : and I must not deny now the publishing of it, (which then I allotted to my private delight) or the publike profit of others. Wherefore though I could plead Custome, the ordinary excuse of all writers, to chuse a *Patron* and protector of their workes, and so shroud my selfe from scandall under your honoura-

A 2
noura-

[31]

nourable favour ; yet have I certaine reasons to excuse this my presumption : First, the many courtesies you have vouchsafed me. Secondly your delightfull skill in matters of this nature. Thirdly, the profit which *I* received from your learned Discourse of Fruit-trees. Fourthly, your animating and assisting of others to such indeavours. Last of all, the rare worke of your own in this kind : All which to publish under your protection, I have adventure d (as you see). Vouchsafe it therefore entertainment, I pray you, and I hope you shall find it not the unprofitablest servant of your retinue. For when your serious employments are over-passed, it may enterpose some commodity, and raise your contentment out of variety.

Your Worships

most bounden,

W ILLIAM LAWSON.

THE

THE PREFACE,
To all well minded.

ART hath her first originall out of Experience, which therefore is called **The School mistrifs of Fools,** *becaufe fhe teacheth infallibly, and plainely, as drawing her knowledge out of the courfe of Nature, (which never fails in the general)by the fenfes, feelingly apprehending, and comparing, (with the help of the Mind) the Workes of Nature; and as in all other things naturall, fo efpecially in Trees. For what is Art more then a provident and skilfull Correctrix of the faults of Nature in particular works, apprehended by the Senfes ? As when good ground naturally brings forth Thiftles, trees ftand too thick, or too thin, or diforderly, or(without dreffing) put forth unproftable Suckers, and fuch-like; all which and a thoufand more, Art reformeth, being taught by Experience: and therefore muft we count that art the fureft, that ftands upon Experimentall Rules, gathered by the rule of Reafon(not Conceit)of all other rules the fureft.*

Whereupon have I, of my meere and fole Experience, without refpect to any former written Treatife, gathered thefe Rules, and fet them down in writing, not daring to hide the leaft talent given me of my Lord and Mafter in heaven. Neither is this injurious to any, though it differ from the common opinion in divers poynts, to make it known to others, what good I have found out, in this faculty by long tryall and experience. I confeffe freely my want of curious skill in the art of planting: and I admire and praife **Plinie, Ariftotle, Virgil, Cicero,** *and*

A 3

many

many others, for wit & judgement in this kind, and leave them to their times, manner, and several Countries.

I am not determined (neither can I worthily) to set forth the praises of this Art; how some, and not a few, even of the best, have accounted it a chiefe part of earthly happinesse, to have fair and pleasant Orchards, as in Hesperia and Thessaly; how all with one consent agree, that it is a chief part of Husbandry, (as Tully de Senectute) and Husbandry maintains the world: how antient, how profitable, how pleasant it is; how many secrets of nature it doth containe, how loved, how much practised in the best places, and of the best. This hath been done by many: I only aim at the common good. I delight not in curious conceits, as planting and graffing with the root upwards, inoculating Roses on Thornes, and such like; although I have heard of diverse, proved some, and read of more.

The Stationer hath (as being most desirous, with me, to further the common good) bestowed much cost and care in having the Knots & Models by the best Artizan cut in great variety, that nothing might be any way wanting to satisfie the curious desire of those that would make use of this Book.

And I shew a plain and sure way of planting, which I have found good by 48 yeeres (and more) experience in the North part of England. I prejudicate and envy none; wishing yet all to abstaine from maligning that good (to them unknown) which is well intended. Farewell.

Thine for thy good,

W. L.

THE

THE BEST, SVRE AND READIEST WAY
TO MAKE A GOOD
Orchard and Garden.

CHAP. I.
Of the Gardner, and his Wages.

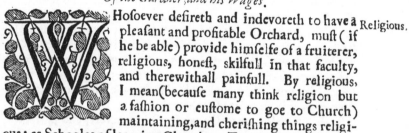 Hofoever defireth and indevoreth to have a Religious. pleafant and profitable Orchard, muft (if he be able) provide himfelfe of a fruiterer, religious, honeft, skilfull in that faculty, and therewithall painfull. By religious, I mean(becaufe many think religion but a fafhion or cuftome to goe to Church) maintaining, and cherifhing things religious: as Schooles of learning; Churches, Tythes, Church goods and rights, and above all things, Gods word, and the preachers thereof, fo much as he is able, practifing prayers, comfortable conferences, mutual inftruction to edifie, almes, and other works of charity, and all out of a good coufcience.

Honefty in a Gardner, will grace your Garden, and all your Honeft. houfe, and help to ftay uubridled Serving-men, giving offence to none, not calling your name into queftion by difhoneft acts, nor infecting your family by evil counfell or example. For there is no plague fo infectious as Popery and Knavery, he will not purloin your profit, nor hinder your pleafures.

Concerning his skill, he muft not be a Sciolift, to make a fhew Skilfull. or take in hand that which he cannot performe, efpecially in fo weighty a thing as an orchard : than the which there can be no human thing more exccellent, either for pleafure or profit, as fhal (God willing) be proved in the treatife following. And what an hindrance fhall it be, not only to the owner, but to the common

mon good, that the unfpeakable benefit of many hundred years fhall be loft, by the audacious attempt of an unskilfull Arborift?

Painfull. The Gardner had not need to be an idle or lazie Lubber, for fo your Orchard, being a matter of fuch moment, will not profper, there will ever be fome thing to doe. Weeds are alwayes growing, the great mother of all living creatures, the Earth, is full of feeds, in her bowels, and any ftirring gives them heat of Sunne, and being laid neer day, they grow: Moales work daily, though not alwaies alike: Winter-hearbs at all times will grow (except in extream froft) In winter your trees and hearbs would be lightned of fnow, and your allies cleanfed : drifts of Snow will fet Deer, Hares, and Conyes, and other noyfome beafts over your walls and hedges into your Orchard. When Summer cloaths your boarders with greene and peckled colours, your Gardner muft dreffe his hedges, and antick workes: watch his bees, and hive them : diftill his Rofes and other Hearbs. Now begin Summer fruits to ripe, and crave your hand to pull them. If he have a Garden (as he muft needs) to keep, you muft needs allow him good help, to end his labours which are endleffe; for no one man is fufficient for thefe things.

Wages. Such a Gardner as will confcionably, quietly and patiently, travell in your Orchard, God fhall crowne the labours of his hands with joyfullneffe, and make the clouds drop fatneffe upon your trees; he will provoke your love, and earne his wages, and fees belonging to his place. The houfe being ferved, fallen fruit, fuperfluity of hearbs, and flowres, feeds, graffes, Sets, and befides all other of that fruit which your bountifull hand fhall reward him withall, will much augment his wages, and the profit of your bees will pay you back againe.

If you be not able, nor willing to hire a gardnor, keep your profits to your felf, but then you muft take all the pains: and for that purpofe (if you want this faculty) to inftruct you, have I undertaken thefe labours, and gathered thefe rules, but chiefly refpecting my countries good.

CHAP.

CHAP. 2.
Of the S y e.

FRuit trees moſt common, and meeteſt for our Northern coun-
tries: (as Apples, Pears, Cherries, Filberds, red and white **Kinds of trees.**
plummes; Damſons Bullis,) for we meddle not with Apricocks
nor Peaches, nor ſcarcely with Quinces, which will not like in
our cold parts, unleſs they be helped with ſome reflex of the ſun
or other like meanes, nor with buſhes bearing berries, as Barberries, Gooſe-berries or Groſers, Raſpe berries, and ſuch like,
though the Barbery be wholeſome, and the tree may be made
great; doe require (as all other trees doe) a black, fat, mellow, **Soyle.**
clean and well tempered ſoyle, wherein they may gather plenty
of good ſap. Some think the Haſell would have a chanily rocke,
and the ſallow, and elder a wateriſh mariſh The ſoyle is made
better by delving and other meanes, being well melted, and the
wildneſſe of the earth and weeds (for every thing ſubject to man
and ſerving his uſe (not well ordered) is by nature ſubject to the
curſe,) is killed by froſt and drought, by fallowing and laying
on heaps and if it be wild earth, with burning.

    If your ground be barren (for ſome are forced to make an Or- **Barren earth.**
chard of barren ground) make a pit three quarters deep, and two
yards wide, and round in ſuch places where you would ſet your
trees, and fill the ſame with fat, pure, and mellow earth, one
whole foot higher then your ſoyle, and therein ſet your plant.
For who is able to manure a whole Orchard plot, if it be barren?
But if you determine to manure the whole ſite, this is your way;
dig a trench halfe a yard deep, all along the lower (if there be a
lower ſide of your Orchard plot, caſting up all the earth on the
inner ſide, and fill the ſame with good, ſh it, hot, and tender
muck; and make ſuch another trench, and fill the ſame as the fiſt
and ſo the third, and ſo throughout your ground : and by this
meanes your plot ſhall be fertile for your life. But be ſure you
ſet your trees neither in dung, nor barren earth.

    Your ground muſt be plain, that it may receive, and keep **Plaine.**
moyſture, not only the rain falling thereon, but alſo water caſt
upon it, or deſcending from higher ground by ſluices, Conduits,
                      B   &c.

&c. For I account moisture in summer very needfull in the soyle of trees, and drought in winter: provided, that the ground be neiher boggy, nor the inundation be past 24 houres at any time, & but twice in the whole Summer and so oft in the winter Therefore if your plot be in a banke or have a descent, make trenches by degrees, Allyes, walkes, and such like, so as the water may be stayed from passage; and if too much water be any hindrance to your walkes (for dry walkes doe well become an Orchard, and an Orchard them) raise your walks with earth first, & then with stones as big as wall-nuts, and lastly, with gravel. In Summer you need not doubt too much water from heaven, either to hurt the health of your body, or your trees. And if over-flowing molest you, after one day, avoid it then by deep trenching.

Moyst.

Some for this purpose dig the soyle of their Orchard, to receive moisture, which I cannot approve: for the roots with digging are oftentimes hurt and especially being digged by some unskilfull servant: for the Gardner cannot doe all himself: and moreover, the roots of Apples and Peares being laid neere day with the heat of the Sun, will put forth suckers, which are a great hinderance, and sometimes with evill guiding, the destruction of trees, unlesse the delving be very shallow, and the ground laid very levell againe. Cherries and Plums, without delving, will hardly or never (after twenty yeares) be kept from such suckers, nor Asps.

Grasse.

Grasse also is thought needfull for moisture, so you let it not touch the rootes of your trees; for it will breed mosse: and the boal of your tree neere the earth, would have the comfort of the Sun and air.

Some take their ground to be too most when it is not so, by reason of water standing thereon; for except in sowre marshes, springs, and continuall over-flowings, no earth can be too moist. Sandy and fat earth will avoid all water falling, by receit: indeed a stiff clay will not receive the water, and therefore if it be grassie or plain, especially hollow, the water will abide, and it will seeme waterish, when the fault is in the want of manuring, and other good dressing.

This plainnesse which we require had need be naturall, because to force any uneven ground, will destroy the fatnesse: for every soyle foyle hath his cruſt next day; wherein trees and hearbs put their roots, and whence they draw their ſap, which is the beſt of the foile, and made fertile with heat and cold, moiſture and drought and under which, by reaſon of the want of the ſaid temperature by the ſaid four qualities, no tree nor hearb (in a manner) will Naturally or can put root : as may be ſeen, if in digging your ground, you plaine. take the weeds of moſt growth, as graſſe or docks (which will grow, though they lye upon the earth bare,) yet bury them under the cruſt, and they will ſurely dye and periſh, and become ma-nure to your ground. This cruſt is not paſt 15 or 18 inches deep in good ground, or other grounds leſſe. Hereby appears the fault of forced plaines, *viz.* your cruſt in the lower parts is covered with the cruſt of the higher parts; and both with worſe earth: Cruſt of the your hights having the cruſt taken away, are become meerly bar- earth. ren : ſo that either you muſt force a new cruſt, or have an evill ſoyle. And be ſure you levell before you plant, leſt you bee forced to remove, or hurt your plants by digging, and caſting among their roots Your ground muſt be cleared, as much as you may, of ſtones and gravell, walls, hedges, buſhes, and other weeds.

CHAP. III.
Of the Site.

THere is no difference, that I find betwixt the neceſſity of a good ſoyl, & a good Site of an Orchard: For a good ſoil (as is before deſcribed) cannot want a good Site ; and if it doe, the fruit cannot be good ; and a good ſite will much amend an evill ſoyle. The beſt ſite is in low grounds, and (if you can) neer unto Low and neere a River. High grounds are not naturally fat.   a River.

And if they have any fatneſſe by mans hand, the very deſcent in time doth waſh it away Tis with grounds in this caſe, as it is with men in a common wealth: Much will have more ; and, Once Poor, ſeldom or never Rich. The Rain will ſcind and waſh, and the wind wil blow fatneſs from the hights to the hollows, where it will abide, and fatten the earth , though it were barren be-fore.

Hence it is, that we have ſeldome any plaine grounds and low, ba rren ; and as ſeldome any hights naturally fertile. It is
B 2 unſpeak-

unspeakable, what fatneffe is brought to low grounds by inundations of waters; neither did I ever know any barren ground in a low plain by a River fide. The goodneffe of the foyle in *Howle* or *Hollowderneffe* in *York-fhire*, is well knowne to all that know the River *Humber*, & the huge bulks of their cattel there. By eftimation of thofe that nave feen the low grounds in *Holland* and *Zealand*, they far furpaffe moft Countries in *Europe* for fruitfulneffe, and only becaufe they lye fo low. The world cannot compare with *Egypt* for fertility, fo far as *Ns us* doth overflow his banks. So that a fitter place cannot be chofen for an Orchard, then a low plain by a River fide. For befides the fatneſs which the water brings, if any cloudy mift or raine be ftirring, it commonly fals down to, and follows the courfe of the River. And where fee we greater trees of bulk and bough, then ftanding on, or neer the water fide? If you afke why the Plaines in *Holdernes* and fuch Countries, are deftitute of woods ? I anfwere, that men and cattle (that have put trees thence, from out of plaines to void corners) are better then trees. Neither are thofe places without trees Our old Fathers can tell us how woods are decayed, & people in the roome of trees multiplyed. I have ftood fomewhat long in this point, becaufe fome doe condemn a moift foil for fruit trees.

Pfal.1.3.
Ezek.17.8.
Ecclus.39.17.
Mr. *Markham*.

A low ground is good to avoid the danger of windes, both for fhaking downe your unripe fruit. Trees (the moft that I know) being loaden with wood for want of proyning, and growing high by the unskilfulneffe of the Arborift, muft needs be in continuall danger of the South Weft, Weft and North-weft winds, efpecially in September and March, when the ayre is moft temperate from extream heat and cold, which are deadly enemies to great winds. VVherefore chufe your ground low : Or if you be forced to plant in a higher ground, let high and ftrong walls, houfes & trees, as wall-nuts, Plane-trees, Oaks and Afhes, placed in good order, be your fence for winds.

The fucken of your dwelling houfe, defcending into your Orchard, if it be cleanly conveyed is good

The Sun, in fome fort, is the life of the world : it maketh proud grouth, and ripens kindly and fpeedily, according to the golden Tearme, *Annus fructificat, non tellus.* Therefore in the

Windes.
Chap. 13.

Sun.

Countries

Countries neerer approaching the Zodiack the Suns habitation, they have better, and sooner rip-fruit, then we that dwel in these frozen parts.

This provoketh most of our great Arborists to plant A- Trees against pricocks, Cherries, and Peaches, by a wall & with racks, & other a wall. means to spread them upon, and fasten them to a wall, to have the benefit of the immoderate reflex of the Sun, which is commendable, for the having of fair, good, and soone ripe fruit. But let them know, it is more hurtfull to their trees then the benefit they reap thereby, as not suffering a tree to live the tenth part of his age; it helps Gardeners to work. For first, the wall hinders the roots ; becaufe into a dry and hard wall of earth or stone, a tree will not, nor cannot put any root to profit, but efpetially it stops the paffage of the fap, whereby the Bark is wounded, and the wood and difeafes grow, fo that the tree becomes short of life. For as in the body of man, the leaning or lying on fome member, whereby the courfe of blood is stopt, makes that member as it were dead for the time, till the blood returne to his courfe, and I think, if that stopping should continue any time, the member will perith for want of blood, (for the life is in the blood) and fo indanger the body ; fo the fap is the life of the tree, as the blood is to mans body : neither doth the tree in winter (as is fuppofed) want his fap, no more then mans body his blood, which in winter, and time of fleep, draws inward : fo that the dead time of winter, to a tree, is but a night of rest : for the tree at all times, even in winter, is nourifh'd with fap and grouth as well as mans body. The chilling cold may well fome little time stay or hinder the proud courfe of the fap, but fo little and fo short a time, that in calm and mild feafons, even in the depth of winter, if you marke it, you may eafily perceive the fap to put out, and your trees to increafe their buds which were formed in the Summer before, and may eafily be difcerned ; for leaves fall not off, till they be thrust off with the knots or buds whereupon it comes topaffe, that trees cannot beare fruit plentifully two yeirs together, and make themfelves ready to Bloffom against the feafonableneffe of the next fpring.

And if any frost be fo extream, that it stay the fap too much, or too long, then it kils the forward fruit in the bud, and fome-

B 3   times

times the tender leaves and twigs, but not the tree : VVherefore to returne, it is perillous to ftop the fap. And where, or when did you ever fee a great tree packt on a wall?Nay, who did ever know a tree fo unkindly fplat,come to age?I have heard of fome that out of their imaginary cunning, have planted fuch trees, on the North fide of the wall,to avoid drought : but the heat of the Sun is as comfortable (which they fhould have regarded) as the drought is hurtfull. And although water is a foveraigne remedy againft drought, yet want of Sun is no way to be helped. Wherefore,to couclude this chapter, let your ground lie fo,that it may have the benefit of the fouth and weft Sun, and fo low and clofe,that it may have moifture,and increafe his fitnefs,(for trees are the greateft fuckers and pillers of the earth) and (as much as may be)free from great winds.

CHAP. IIII.
Of the Quantity.

IT would be remembred what a benefit rifeth, not onely to every particular owner of an Orchard, but alfo to the common wealth by fruit,as fhall be fhewed in the fixteenth chapter (God willing);whereupon muft needs fallow, the greater the Orchard is(being good, & well kept)the better it is : for of good things, being equally good, the biggeft is the beft. And if it fhall appear,that no ground a man occupieth, (no, not the Corn field) yeeldeth more gaine to the purfe, and houfe-keeping(not to

Orchard as good as a Corne field.

fpeak of the unfpeakable pleafure)quantity for quantity, then a good Orchard, (befides, the coft in planting and dreffing an Orchard is not fo much by far, as the labour and Seeding of your Corn fields nor for durance of time comparable , befides the certainty of the one before the other) I fee not how any labour or coft in this kind, can be idly or waftfully beftowed, or thought too much And what other thing is a Vineyard,in thofe Countries where Vines doe thrive, then a large Orchard of trees bearing fruit?or what difference is there in the juyce of the

Compared with a Vineyard.

Grape, and our Sider and perry, but the goodneffe of the foil, and clime where they gow ? which maketh the one more ripe, and fo more pleafant then the other. Whatfoever can be faid for

the

the benefit riſing from an Orchard, that makes for the largneſſe of the Orchard bounds. And me thinks they doe prepoſterouſly, that beſtow more coſt and labour, and more ground in and upon a Garden, then upon an orchard, whence they reap and may reap both more pleaſure and more profit, by infinite degrees. And further, that a Garden never ſo freſh, and fair, and well kept, cannot continue without both renewing of the earth and the hearbs often, in the ſhort and ordinary age of a man : whereas your Orchard well kept, ſhall dure divers hundred yeeres, as ſhall be ſhewed *chap* 14. In a large orchard there is much labour ſaved, in fencing and otherwiſe: for three little orchards or a few trees, being in a manner all out-ſides, are ſo blaſted and dangered, and commonly in keeping neglected, and require a great fence ; whereas in a great orchard, trees are a mutuall fence one to another, and the keeping is regarded ; and leſſe fencing ſerves ſix acres together, then three in ſeverall incloſures.

margin: Compared with a Garden.

Now what quantity of ground is meeteſt for an Orchard can no man preſcribe, but that muſt be left to every mans ſeverall judgement, to be meaſured according to his ability & will, for other neceſſaries beſides fruit muſt be had, and ſome are more delighted with orchards then others.

margin: What quantity of ground.

Let no man, having a fit plot, plead poverty in this caſe ; for an orchard once planted, will maintain it ſelf, and yeeld infinite profit beſide. And I am perſwaded, that if men did know the right and beſt way of planting, dreſſing, and keeping trees, and felt the profit and pleaſure thereof, both they that have no orchards, would have them, and they that have orchards would have them larger, yea fruit trees in their hedges, as in Worceſter-ſhire, &c. And I think, the want of planting is a great loſſe to our common wealth, and in particular, to the owners of Lordſhips, which Landlords themſelves might eaſily amend, by granting longer time and better aſſurance to their tenants, who have taken up this Proverb, *Botch and ſit, Build and flit* : for who will build or plant for another mans profit ? Or the Parliament might injoyne every occupier of grounds to plant and maintaine for ſo many acres of fruitfull ground, ſo many ſeverall trees, or kinds of trees for fruit. Thus much for quantity.

margin: Want is no hindrance.

margin: How Landlords by their Tenants may make flouriſhing Orchards in England.

CHAP.

A. All thefe fquares muft bee fet with trees, the Gardens and other ornaments muft ftand in fpaces betwixt the trees, and in the borders and fences.

B. Trees 20. yards a funder.

C. Garden Knots.

D. Kitchin Garden.

E. Bridge.

F. Conduit.

G. Staires.

H. Walkes fet with great wood thick.

I. VValkes fet with great wood round about your Orchard

K. The Out fence.

L. The Out fence fet with ftone fruit.

M. Mount. To force earth for a Mount of fuch like, fet it round with quick and lay boughes of trees ftrangely intermingled, the tops inward, with the earth in the midd'e.

N. Still-houfe.

O. Good ftanding for Bees, if you have an houfe.

P. If the river run by your doore, and under your Mount it will be pleafant.

CHAP. V.
Of the Form.

THe goodneſſe of the ſoil and ſite, are neceſſary to the well-being of an Orchard ſimply, but the form is ſo far neceſſary, as the owner ſhall think meet. For that kind of form wherewith every particular man is delighted, we leave it to himſelfe, *Suum cuique pulchrum.* The form that men like in generall, is a ſquare: for although roundneſſe be *forma perfectiſsima*, yet that principle is good, where neceſſity by art doth not force ſome other form. It within one large ſquare the Gardiner ſhall make one round Labyrinth or Maze with ſome kind of Berries, it will grace your form, ſo there be ſufficient roome left for walkes, ſo will four or more round knots do, for it is to be noted that the eye muſt be pleaſed with the forme. I have ſeene ſquares riſing by degrees with ſtays from your houſe ward, according to this forme which I have *Craſſa quod aiunt Minerva*, with an unſteady hand, rough hewen: for in forming Countrie gardens, the better ſort may uſe better formes, and more coſtly worke. What is needfull more to be ſaid, I referre all that (concerning the form) to the Chapter 17. of the Ornaments of an Orchard.

The uſuall forme is a ſquare.

CHAP. VI.
Of Fences.

ALL your labour paſt and to come about an Orchard is loſt, unleſſe you fence well. It ſhall grieve you much to ſee your young ſets rubd looſe at the roots, the bark pild, the boughs and twigs cropt, your fruit ſtolne, your trees broken, and your many years labours and hopes deſtroyed, for want of fences. A chiefe care muſt be had in this point: you muſt therefore plant in ſuch a ſoile, where you may Provide a convenient, ſtrong, and ſeemly fence. For you can poſſeſſe no goods, that have ſo many enemies as an orchard, looke Chapter 13. Fruits are ſo delightſome, and deſired of ſo many (nay in a manner of all) and yet few will be at coſt and take pains to provide them. Fence well therefore, let your plot be wholly in your owne power, that you

Effects of evill fencing.

C make

Let the fence be your own. make all your fence your selfe : for neighbours fence is none at all, or very carelesse. Take heed of a doore or window,(yea of a wall)of any other mans into your orchard : yea,though it be nailed up, or the wall be high , for perhaps they will prove theeves.

Kinds of Fences; earthen walles. All fences commonly are made of earth, Stone, Bricke,wood, or both earth and wood . Dry wall of earth, and dry ditches are the worst fences save pales or railes,and doe wast the soonest,unlesse they be well copt with Glooe and morter , whereon at Michaell tide it will be good to sow wall-flowers ; commonly called Bee flowers, or winter Gillyflowers, because they will grow (though among stones)and abide the strongest frost and drought continually greene and flowring even in winter,and have a pleasant smell,and are timely, (that is they will flower the first and the last of flowers)and are good for Bees.And your earthen wall is good for bees dry and warme but these fences are both unseemly, evill to repaire, and onely for need, where stone or wood cannot be had. Whosoever makes such walls,must not pill the ground in the Orchard , for getting earth , nor make any pits or hollowes, which are both unseemly and unprofitable : old dry earth mixt with sand is best for these.This kind of wall will soone decay by reason of the trees which grow neer it,for the roots and boals of great trees,will increase, undermine,and over-turne such walls, though they were of stone, as is apparent by Ashe s,Round-trees, Burt-trees, and such like, carried in the chat, or berry, by birds into stone walls.

Pale & Raile. Fences of dead wood,as pales,will not last,neither will railes either last or make good fence.

Stone walls. Stone walls(where stone may be had)are the best of this sort both for fencing, lasting,and shrouding of your young trees but about this you must bestow much Paines and more cost, to have them handsome,high and durable.

Quick wood and Moats. But of all other(in mine opinion)Quickwood and moates or ditches of water, where the ground is levell, is the best fence . In unequall grounds, which will not keep water, there a double ditch may be cast, made streight and levell on the top two yards broad for a fair walk, five or six foot higher then the soil,with a gutter on either side,two yards wide,& four foot deep,set without with three or four chesse of thorns,and within with cherrys,

Plummes

Plummes,Damſon,Bullys,Filberds, (for I love thoſe trees better for their fruit,and as well for their form, as privit,)for you may make them take any forme.And in every corner,(and middle if you will)a mount would be raiſed, whereabout the wood may claſpe, poudered with wood-binde: which will make with dreſſing a faire, pleaſant, profitable,and ſure fence. But you muſt be ſure that your quick thorns either grow wholly, or that there be a ſupply betime, either planting new, or plaſhing the old where need is. And aſſure your ſelfe, that neither wood, ſtone, earth , nor water , can make ſo ſtronga fence, as this ſeven at years grouth.

Moates, Fiſh ponds, and(eſpecially at one ſide,a River)with- Moates. in and without your fence, will afford you fiſh, fence, and moiſture to your trees;and pleaſure alſo, if they be ſo great and deep that you may have Swans, and other water birds, good for devouring of vermine, and boat for many good uſes.

It ſhall hardly availeyou to make any fence for your Orchard , if you be a niggard of your fruit . For as liberality will ſave it beſt from noiſome neighbours,(liberalitie I ſay is the beſt fence) ſo juſtice muſt reſtraine rioters. Thus when your ground is tempered,ſquared,and fenced it is time to provide for planting.

CHAP. VII
Of Sets.

THere is not onepoint (in my opinion) about an Orchard more to be regarded, then the choiſe getting and ſetting of good plants , either for readineſſe of having good fruit , or for continuall laſting for whoſoever ſhall fail in the choiſe of good ſets, or in getting,or gathering or ſetting his plants, ſhall never have agood or laſting Orchard. And I take want of skill in this faculty,tobe a cheif hinderance to the moſt Orchards , and to many for having Orchards at all.

Some for readineſſe uſe ſlips, which ſeldome take root, and Slips. if they doe take,they cannot laſt, both becauſe their root having a maine wound will in ſhort time decay the body of the tree : and beſides, that roots being ſo weakly put , are ſoone nipt with drought or froſt, I could never ſee(lightly)any ſlip,but of apples onely,ſet for trees.

C 2   A

Bur-knot. A Bur-knot kindly taken from an apple-tree, is much better and surer. You must cut him close at the root end, an handfull under the knot (some use in Summer about Lammas to circumcise him and put earth to the knots with hay-ropes, and in winter cut him off and set him; but this is curiosity needlesse, & danger with removing and drought) and cut away all his twigs save one, the most principall, which in setting you must leave above the earth, burying his trunck in the cruft of the earth for his root It matter not much what part of the bough the twigs grows out of. If it grow out of, or neer the root end, some say such an aple will have no core nor kernel. O, if it p eafe the planter he may let his bough be crooked, and leave out his top end one foot, or somewhat more, wherein will be good grafting; if either you like not, or doubt the fruit of the bough, (for commonly your bur-knots are Summer fruit) or if you think he will not, recover his wound fafely

Ufuall fets. The moft ufuall kind of Sets are plants with roots growing, of kernels of apples, Pears, and Crabbs, or ftones of Cherries, Plums, &c. removed out of a nurfery, wood, or other Orchard, into, and fet, in your Orchard in due places. I grant this kind to be better then either of the other by much, as more fure and more **Maine roots cut.** durable. Herein you muft note, that in Sets fo removed, you get all the roots you can, and without bruifing of any. I utterly diflike the opinion of thofe great gardners, that following their books, would have the maine roots cut away: for tops cannot **Srow fets removed.** grow without roots. And becaufe none can get all the roots, and removal is an hinderance, you may not leave on all tops, when you fet them: For there is a proportion betwixt the top and root of a tree, even in the number (at leaft in the growth) If the roots be many, they will bring you many tops, if they be not hindered. And if you ufe to ftow or top your tree too much or too low, and leave no iffue, or little for fap, (as is to be feen in your hedges) it will hinder the growth of roots and boal, becaufe fuch a kind of ftowing is a kind of fmothering or choaking the fap. Great wood, as Oak, Elm, Afh, &c. being continually kept down with fheer knife, ax, &c. neither boal nor root will thrive, but as an hedg or bufh. If you intend to graff in your fets, you may cut him cloffer with a greater wound, and neerer the earth with-

within a foot or two , becaufe the graft or grafts will cover his
wound. If you like his fruit, and would have him to be a tree of
himfelfe , be not fo bold. This I can tell you , that though you
do cut his top clofe , and leave nothing but his bulke , becaufe
his roots are few, if he be (but little) bigger then your thumb (as
I wifh all plants removed to be (he will fafely recover his wound
within feven yeers, by good guidance , that is, if the next time
of dreffing, immediately above his uppermoft fprig, you cut him
off aflope cleanly, fo that the fprig ftand on the back fide, (and
if you can Northward, that the wound may have the benefit of
the Sun) at the upper end of the wound; and let that fprig onely be the boal . And take this for a generall rule ; Every young Generall rule.
plant, if he thrive, will recover any wound above the earth, by
good dreffing, although it be to the one halfe , and to his very
heart. This fhort cutting at the remove , faves your plants from
wind and needs the leffe or no ftaking. I commend not lying or Tying of trees.
leaning of trees againft holds or ftays ; for it breede obftruction
of fap, and wounds incurable. All removing of trees as great as Generall rule.
your arm, or above, is dangerous ; though fome time fuch will
grow, but not continue long, becaufe they be tainted with deadly wounds, either in the root or top (and a tree once thorowly
tainted, is never good.) And though they get fome hold in the Signes of dif-
eafes, chap. 13.
earth with fome leffer taw or taws, which give fome nourifh-
ment to the body of the tree; yet the heart being tainted , he
will hardly ever thrive ; which you may eafily difcern by the
blackneffe of the boughs as the heart, when you dreff your trees.
Alfo, when he is fet with more tops then the roots can nourifh;
the tops decaying, blacken the boughs, and the boughs the arms,
and fo they boil at the very heart. Or this taint in the removall,
if it kill not prefently, but after fome fhort time it may be difcerned, blackneffe or yellowneffe in the bark, and a fmall
hungred leaf. Or if your removed plant put forth leaves the next
and fecond Summer, and little or few fprafes , is a great fign of
a taint , and next years death. I have known a tree tainted in
fetting, yet grow, and beare bloffomes for divers years; and
yet for want of ftrength could never fhape his fruit.

Next unto this, or rather equall with thefe plants, are fuck- Suckets good
ers growing out of the roots of great trees, which Cherries and fets.
C 3   Plums

Plums do feldome or never want and being taken kindly with
their roots, will make very good fets. And you may help them
much by enlarging their roots with the taws of the tree whence
you take them They are of two forts : Either growing from the
very root of the tree : and here you muft be carefull, not to
hurt your tree when you gather them, by ripping amongft the
roots; and that you take them clean away : for thefe are a great
and continuall annoyance to the grouth of your tree; and they
will hardly be cleanfed . Secondly, or they doe arife from fome
taw : and thefe may be taken without danger, with long and
good roots and will foone become trees of ftrength.

A Running
plant.

　　There is another way, which I have not thorowly proved, to
get not onely plants for graffing, but Sets to remain for trees,
which I call a *Running plant*: the manner of it is this: Take a root
or kirnell, & put into the middle of your plot; & the fecond yeere
in the fpring geld his top, if he have one principall (as commonly
by nature they have) & let him put forth only four Syons toward
the four corners of the Orchard, as neer the earth as you can. If
he put not four (which is rare) ftay his top till he have put fo many. When you have four fuch, cut the ftock aflope, as is aforefaid
in this Chapter. hard above the uppermoft fprig, and keep thofe
four without Syons clean and ftreight till you have them a yard
and a half, at leaft, or two yards long . Then the next fpring, in
graffing time, lay down thofe four fprays, towards the four corners of you r Orchard, with their tops in a heap of pure and good
earth, and raifed as high as the root of your Syon, (for fap will
not defcend) & a fod to keep them down, leaving nine or twelve
inches of the top to looke upward In that hill he will put roots,
and his top new cyons, which you muft fpread as before, and fo
from hill to hill, till he fpread the compaffe of your ground, or
as far as you lift. If, in bending the Syons crack, the matter is
fmall; cleanfe the ground, and he will recover. Every bended
bough will put forth branches, and become trees. If this plant
be of a bur knot, there is no doubt: I have proved it in one branch
my felfe, and I know at *Wilton* in *Cleveland*, a Pear-tree of a
great bulke and age, blowne clofe to the earth, hath put at every
knot roots into the earth, and from root to top, a great number
of mighty armes or trees, filling a great room, like many trees, or

a

a little Orchard. Much better may it be done by Art, in a lelſe
tree. And I could not miſlike this kind, ſave that time will be
long before it come to perfection.

Many uſe to buy ſets already grafted; which is not the beſt way: Sets bought.
for firſt, all removes are dangerous : again there is danger in the
carriage. Thirdly, it is a coſtly courſe of planting : Fourthly,
every Gardner is not truſty to ſell you good fruit : Fifthly, you
know not which is beſt, which is worſt, and ſo may take moſt
care about your worſt trees. Laſtly, this way keeps you from
practiſe, and ſo from experience, in ſo Good, Gentlemanly,
Scholerlike, and profitable a faculty.

The onely beſt way (in my opinion) to have ſure and laſting The beſt ſets.
ſets, is never to remove: for every remove is a hinderance, if not Vnremoved
a dangerous hurt, or deadly taint. This is the way : The plat- how.
form being laid, and the plot appoynted where you will plant
every Set in your Orchard, dig the roome where your ſet ſhall
ſtand, a yard compaſſe, & make the earth mellow and clean, and
mingle it with a few cole-aſhes, to avoid worms: and immediatly after the firſt change of the Moone, in the latter end of *Februa-*
ry, the earth being afreſh turned over, put in every ſuch room
three or four kirnels of Apples or peares of the beſt; every kirnell
in an hole made with your finger, finger-deep, a foot diſtant
one from another; and that day month following, as many more,
(leaſt ſome of the former miſſe) in the ſame compaſs, but not in
the ſame holes. Hence (God willing) ſhall you have roots enough:
If they all or divers of them come up, you may draw (but not
dig) up (nor put down) at your pleaſure, the next *November.* How
many ſoever you take away, to give or beſtow elſewhere, be ſure
to leave two of the proudeſt. And when in your ſecond or third
yeer you graff, if you graff then at all, leave the one of thoſe two
ungraffed, leſt in graffing the other, you fail. For I find by tryall,
that after the firſt or ſecond graffing in the ſame ſtock, being miſt
(for who hits all?) the third miſſe puts your ſtock in deadly
danger, for want of iſſue of ſap. Yea, though you hit in graffing,
yet may your graffs with wind or otherwiſe be broken down. If
your graffs or graff proſper, you have your deſire, in a plant unremoved, without taint, and the fruit at your owne choice : and
ſo you may (ſome little earth being removed) pull but not dig
up

up the other plant or plants in that room. If your graff or ftock, or both perifh, you have another in the fame place , of better ftrength to work upon; for thriving without fnub, he will over lay your grafted ftock much. And it is hardly poffible to miffe in grafting fo often, if your gardiner be worth his name.

Sets ungrafted beft of all.   It fhall not be amiffe (as I judge it) if your kernels be of choice fruit, and that you fee them come forward proudly in their body, and beare a fair and broad leaf in colour , tending to a greenifh yellow, (which argues pleafant and great fruit) to try fome of them ungrafted: for although it be a long time ere this come to bear fruit, ten or twelve years, or more; and at their firft bearing, the fruit will not feem to be like his owne kind, yet am I affured, upon tryall, before twenty years grouth, fuch trees will increafe the bigneffe and goodneffe of their fruit and come perfectly to their owne kind . Trees (like other breeding creatures) as they grow in yeers, bigneffe and ftrength, fo they mend their fruit. Husbands and houfwives find this true by experience , in the rearing of their young ftore. More then this, there is no tree like this for foundneffe and durable laft, if his keeping and dreffing be anfwerable. I grant, the readieft way to come foone to fruit, is graffing ; becaufe, in a manner, all your graffs are taken off fruit-bearing trees.

Time of removing.   Now when you have made choife of your fets to remove, the ground being ready , the beft time is, immediatly after the fall of the leaf, in or about the change of the Moon, when the fap is moft quiet. for then the fap is turning : for it makes no ftay, but in the *extremity* of drought or cold· At any time in winter, may *Generall rule.* you tranfplant trees , fo you put no ice nor fnow to the root of your plant in the fetting : and therefore open, calm, and moift weather is beft To remove, the leaf being ready to fall and not fallen, or buds apparently put forth in a moift warm feafon, for need, fometime may do well ; but the fafeft is to walk in the plain troden path.

Some hold opinion, that it is beft removing before the fall of the leaf; and I hear it is commonly practifed in the South by our beft Arborifts, the leaf not fallen; & they give the reafon to be, that the defcending of the fap will make fpeedy roots . But mark the reafons following and I think you fhall find no foundneffe either

in

in that pofition or practice, at leaft in the reafon.

1. I fay, it is dangerous to remove when the fap is not quiet; for every remove gives a main check to the ftirring fap, by ftaying the courfe thereof in the body of your plant, as may appear by trees removed any time in Summer, they commonly die, nay hardly fhall you fave the life of the moft young and tender plant of any kind of wood (fcarcely hearbs) if you remove them in the pride of fap : for proud fap univerfally ftayed by removal, ever hinders, often taints, and fo prefently, or in very fhort time, kills. Sap is like blood in mans body, in which is the life, *cap* 3 *p* 9. If the blood univerfally be cold, life is excluded : fo is fap tainted by untimely removal. A ftay by drought, or cold, is not fo dangerous (though dangerous, if it be extreame) becaufe more natural.

2. The fap never defcends, as men fuppofe; but is confolidated and tranfubftantiated into the fubftance of the tree, and paffeth (alwaies above the earth) upward, not onely betwixt the bark and the wood, but alfo into and in both body and bark, though not fo plentifully, as may appear by a tree budding, nay fructifying two or three yeers, after he be circumcifed, at the very root, like a River that enlargeth his chanel by a continual defcent.

3. I cannot perceive what time they would have the fap to defcend. At *Midfummer* in a biting drought it ftays, but defcends not; for immediately upon moifture, it makes fecond fhoots, as (or before rather) *Michaeltide*, when it fhapens his buds for next yeers fruit. If at the fall of leaf, I grant, about that time is the greateft ftand, but no defcent of fap, which begins fomewhat before the leaf fall, but not long ; therefore at that time muft be the beft removing, not by reafon of defcent, but ftay of fap.

4. The fap in this courfe hath its profitable and apparent effects; as the growth of the tree, covering of wounds, putting of buds, &c whereupon it follows, if the fap defcend, it muft needs have fome effect to fhew it.

5. Laftly, boughs plafht and laid lower then the root, die for want of fap defcending, except where it is forced by the main ftream of the fap, as in top boughs hanging like water in pipes, or except the plafht boughs lying on the ground put roots of his own; yea under-boughs, which we commoly call water-boughs

D   can

can scarcely get sap to live, yea in time die, because the sap doth presse so violently upward , and therefore the fairest shoots and fruits are always in the top·

Remove soon.   *Object.* If you say that many so removed thrive; I say, that somewhat before the fall of the leaf (but not much) is the stand ; for the fall and the stand are not at one instant: before the stand, is dangerous But to returne.

The sooner in winter you remove your sets the better; the latter the worse: for it is very perillous if a strong drought take your sets before they have made good their rooting. A plant set at the fall, (shall gain (in a manner)a whole yeers growth of that which is set in the spring after.

The manner of setting,   I use in the setting to be sure that the earth be mouldy,(and somewhat moist) that it may run among the small tangles without straining or bruising : and as I fill in earth to his root , I shake the Set easily too and fro, to make the earth settle the better to his roots ; and withall easily with my foot I put in the earth close ; for Ayre is noysome, and concavities will follow. Some prescribe Oats to be put in with the earth I could like it, if I could know any reason thereof. And they use to set their plants with the same side towards the Sun; but this conceit is like the other. For first, I would have every tree to stand so free from shade , that not onely the root (which therfore you must keep bare from grasse)but body , boughs, and branches , and every spray, may have the benefit of the Sun· And what hurt, if that part of the tree which before was shadowed , be now made partaker of the heat of the Sun? In turning of Bees I know it is hurtfull, because it changeth their entrance, passage, and whole work but not so in trees.

Set in the crust.   Set as deep as you can, so that in any wise you goe not beneath the crust. Look *Chap* 2.

Moysture good   Wee spake in the second Chapter of moisture in general : but now especially having put your removed plant into the earth , powre on water (of a puddle were good)by distilling presently, and so every week twice, in strong drought, so long as the earth will drink, and refuse by overflowing. For moisture mollifies, and both gives leave to the roots to spread , and maks the earth yeeld sap and nourishment with plenty and facility. Nurses, they

(they say)give beft and moft milk after warm drinks.

If your ground be fuch, that it will keep no moifture at the root of your plant,fuch plants fhall never like, or but for a time. There is nothing more hurtfull for young trees, then piercing drought. I have knowne trees of good ftature, after they have been of divers years growth,and thrive well for a good time, perifh for want of water,and very many by reafon of taints in fetting.

It is meet your fets and grafts be fenced, till they be as big as your arm, for fear of annoyances. Many ways may Sets receive damages, after they be fet, whether grafted or ungrafted. For although we fuppofe, that no noyfome beaft or other thing muft have acceffe among your trees; yet by cafualty, a Dog, Cat,or fuch like,or your felf; or negligent freind bearing you company, or a fhrewd boy,may tread or fall upon a young and tender plant or graft. To avoid thefe and many fuch chances, you muft ftake them round a pretty diftance from the Set, neither fo near nor fo thick, but that it may have the benefit of the Sun, Rain, and Air. Your ftakes(fmall or great) would be fo furely put, or driven into the earth, that they break not, if any thing happen to lean upon them, elfe may the fall be more hurtfull then the want of the fence. Let not your ftakes fhelter any weeds about your fets; for want of Sun is a great hinderance. Let them ftand fo far off, that your grafts fpreading receive no hurt, either by rubbing on them, or of any other thing paffing by. If your ftock be long, and high grafted,(which I muft difcommend, except in need) becaufe there the fap is weak, and they are fubject to ftrong winds,and the lightings of birds,) tie eafily with a foft lift three or four pricks, under the clay, and let their tops ftand above the grafts to avoid the lighting of Crowes, Pies, &c.upon your grafts. If you ftick fome fharp thorns at the roots of your ftalks, they will make hurtfull things keep off the better. Other better fences for your grafts I know none. And thus much for fets and fetting.

(margin note: Grafts muft be fenced.)

CHAP.VIII.
Of the diftance of trees.

I Know not to what end you fhould provide good ground, well fenced,and plant good fets;and when your trees fhould come

D 2 to

to profit, have all your labours loſt, for want of due regard to
the diſtance of placing your trees. I have ſeen many trees ſtand ſo
thick, that one could not thrive for the throng of his neighbours.

Hurts of too neere planting. If you do mark it, you ſhall ſee the tops of trees rubbed off, their
ſide galled like a gall'd horſe back ; and many trees have more
ſtumps then boughs, and moſt trees not well thriving, but ſhort,
ſtumpiſh, and evill-thriving boughs; like a Corn-field overſeed-
ed, or a Town over peopled, or a paſture over laid; which the
Gardner muſt either let grow, or leave the Tree very few boughs
to bear fruit. Hence ſmall thrift, galls, wounds, diſeaſes, and
ſhort life to the trees : and while they live, green, little, hard,
worm-eaten, and evill-thriving fruit ariſe, to the diſcomfort of
the owners.

    To prevent which diſcommodity, one of the beſt remedies is,
the ſufficient and fit diſtance of trees. Therefore at the ſetting of
your plants, you muſt have ſuch reſpect, that the diſtance of them
be ſuch, that every tree be not annoyance, but an help to his fellowes : for trees (as all other things of the ſame kind) ſhould
ſhroud, and not hurt one another. And aſſure your ſelf, that every
touch of trees (as well under as above) is hurtfull : Therefore this
Generall rule muſt be a general rule in this Art, That no tree in an Orchard
All touches hurtfull. well ordered, nor no bough, nor cyon, drop upon or touch his
fellowes. Let no man think this impoſſible, but look in the
eleventh Chapter of dreſſing of trees. If they touch, the wind will
cauſe a forcible rub. Young twigs are tender, if boughs or arms
touch or rub, if they are ſtrong, they make great galls. No kind of
touch therefore in trees can be good.

The beſt di- Now it is to be conſidered what diſtance among Sets is requi-
ſtance of trees ſite, and that muſt be gathered from the compaſſe and room that
each tree by probability will take and fill. And herein I am of a
contray opinion to all them which practiſe or teach the planting of trees, that ever yet I knew, read or heard of: for the common ſpace betwene tree and tree, is ten foot; if twenty foot, it is
thought very much. But I ſuppoſe 20 yards diſtance is ſmall e-
nough betwixt tree and tree, or rather too too little. For the
diſtance muſt needs be as far as two trees are well able to over-
ſpread and fill, ſo they touch not by one yard at the leaſt. Now I
am aſſured, and I know one Apple tree, ſet of a ſlip *finger-great*,
in

in the space of twenty years (which I account a very small part of a trees age, as is shewed chap. 14.) hath spread his boughes eleven or twelve yards compasse that is, five or sixe yards on every side. Hence I gather, that in forty or fifty years, (which yet is but a small time of his age)a tree in good soile, well liking, by good dressing (for that is much availeable to this purpose) will spread double at the least, viz. twelve yards on a side; which being added to twelve allotted to his fellow make twenty and foure yards, and so farre distant must every tree stand from another. And look how far a tree spreads his boughs above, so far doth he put his roots under the earth, or rather further, if there be no stop nor let by walls, trees, rocks, barren earth, and such-like for an huge bulke, and strong armes, massie boughes, many branches, and infinite twigs, re- The parts of quire wide spreading roots. The top hath the vast aire to a tree- spread his boughes in, high and low, this way and that way; but the roots are kept in the crust of the earth, they may not goe downeward, nor upward out of the earth, which is their element, no more then the fish out of the water, Camelion out of the aire, nor Salamander out of the fire. Therefore they must needs spread far under the earth. And I dare well say, If Nature would give leave to man, by Art to dresse the root of trees, to take away the taws and tangles that lap and fret, and grow superfluously and disorderly, (for every thing *sublunary* is cursed for mans sake) the tops above being answerably dressed, we should have trees of wonderfull greatnesse, and infinite durance. And I perswade my selfe that this might be done sometimes in winter, to trees standing in faire plains and kindly earth, with small or no danger at all. So that I conclude, that twenty foure yards is the least space that Art can allow for trees to stand distant one from another.

If you aske me what use shall be made of that wast ground Wast groud betwixt tree and tree: I answer, If you please to plant some in an Or- tree or trees in that middle space, you may; and as your trees chard. grow contiguous, great and thick, you may at your pleasure take up those last trees. And this I take to be the chiefe cause why the most trees stand so thick: for men not knowing (or not regarding) this secret of needfull distance, and loving

fruit

fruit of trees planted to their hands, think much to pull up any though they pine one another. If you or your heirs or fuccef-forts would take up fome great trees (paft fetting) where they ftand too thick, be fure to doe it about Midfomer, and leave no maine roots. I deftinate the fpace of foure and twenty yards, for trees of age and ftature. More then this , you have borders to be made for walks, with Rofes, Berries; &c.

And chiefly confider, that your Orchard, for the firft twenty or thirty years, will ferve you for many Gardens; for Saffron, Licoras, roots, and other hearbs for profit, and flowers for plea-fure : fo that no ground need be wafted if the Gardiner be skil-full and diligent. But be fure you come not neere with fuch deep delving the roots of your trees, whofe compaffe you may partly difcerne, by the compaffe of the tops, if your top be well fpread. And under the droppings and fhadow of your trees, be fure no hearbs will like. Let this be faid for the diftance of trees.

CHAP. IX.
Of the placing of Trees.

THe placing of trees in an Orchard, is well worth the regard: For although it muft be granted , that any of ourforefaid trees (chap. 2.) will like well in any part of your Orchard, be-ing good and well dreft earth ; yet are not all trees alike wor-thy of a good place. And therefore I wifh that your Filbert, Plums, Damfons, Bulleffe, and fuch like be utterly removed from the plain foyle of your Orchard into your fence: for there is not fuch fertility and eafefull growth, as within : and there alfo they are more fubject to, & can abide the blafts of *Æolus.* The Cherries and Plums being ripe in the hot time of Summer, and the reft ftanding longer, are not fo foon fhaken as your better fruit: nei-ther, if they fuffer loffe, is your loffe fo great. Befides that, your fences and ditches will devour fome of your fruit growing in, or neare your hedges. And feeing the continu-ance of all thefe (except Nuts) is fmall, the care of them ought to be the leffe. And make no doubt, but the fences of a large Or-chard will containe a fufficient number of fuch kind of Fruit-trees in the whole compaffe. It is not materiall, but at your pleafure; in the faid fences, you may either intermingle
your

your severall kinds of Fruit-trees; or set every kind by it selfe, order doth very well become your better & greater fruit Let therefore your Apples, Peares, and Quinces, possesse the soile of your
Orchard, unlesse you be especially affected to some of your
other kinds: and of them, let your greatest trees of growth stand
further from Sun, and your Quinces at the south side or end, and
your Apples in the middle: so shall none bee any hindrance to
his fellows. The warden tree, and Winter-peare will challenge
the preeminence for stature. Of your Apple-trees, you shall find
a difference in growth. A good Pippin will grow large, and a
Costard-tree: stead them on the North-side of your other Apples; thus being placed, the least will give Sun to the rest, and
the greatest will shroud their fellows. The Fences and out-trees
will guard all.

CHAP X.
Of Grafting.

NOw are we come to the most curious point of our facul- Of Graving
ty. curious in conceit, but in deede as plaine and easie as or Carving.
the rest, when it is plainly shewn, which we commonly call Graf- Grafting what

fing

Grafting what. fing,or(after fome)Grafting,I cannot Etymologize,nor fhew the originall of the Word,except it come of Graving or Carving.

But the the thing or matter is: The reforming of the fruit of one tree with the fruit of another, by an artificiall tranfplacing or tranfpofing of a twigge,bud or leafe,(commonly called a **A Graffe.** Graft) taken from one tree of the fame, or fome other kinde, and placed or put to, or into another tree in one time and manner.

Kinds of grafting. Of this there be divers kinds, but three or foure now efpecially in ufe : to wit, Grafting, incifing, packing on, grafting in the fcutchion, or inoculating · whereof the chiefe and moft ufuall, is called Grafting (by the generall name, *Catexochen* : (for it is the moft known, fureft, readieft, and plaineft way to have ftore of good fruit.

Graft how. It is thus wrought; You muft with a fine, thin, ftrong and fharpeSaw, made and armed for that purpofe, cut off a foot above the ground, or thereabouts, in a plain without a knot, or as neare as you can without a knot (for fome ftocks will bee knotty) your Stocke, fet,or plant being furely ftayed with your foot and legg ; or otherwife ftraight overwhart (for the Stock may be crooked) and then plain his wound fmoothly with a fharpe knife : that done, cleave him cleanly in the middle with a cleaver,and a knock or mall,and with a wedge of Wood, Iron, or Bone , two handful long at leaft; put into the middle of that clift,with the fame knock,make the wound gape a ftraw breadth wide into which you muft put your Graffes.

A graft what. The graft is a top-twig taken from fome other tree (for it is a folly to put a graffe into his owne ftock) beneath the uppermoft (and fometimes in need,the fecond) knot, and with a fharp knife fitted in the knot (and fometimes out of the knot when need is) with fhoulders an inch downward, and fo put into the ftock with fome thrufting (but not ftraining) barke to barke inward.

Eyes. Let your graffe have three or four eyes for readines to put forth, and give iffue to the fap.It is not amiffe to cut off the top of your graffe,& leave it but five, or fixe inches long, becaufe commonly you fhall fee the tops of long graffes die. The reafon is this.The fap in graffing receives a rebuke,& cannot worke fo ftrongly prefently, sently and your graffs receive not sap so readily, as the naturall branches. When your graffs are cleanly & closely put in, & your wedge puld out nimbly, for fear of putting your graffs out of frame, take well tempered morter, soundly wrought with chaffe or horse dung (for the dung of cattle will grow hard, and straine your graffs) the quantity of a Goose egge, and divide it Just, and therewith all cover your stock, laying the one halfe on the one side and the other halfe on the other side of your graffes, (lest thrusting again your graffes you move them) and let both your hands thrust at once, and alike, and let your clay be tender, to yeeld easily; and all, lest you move your graffes. Some use to cover the cleft of the stocke, under the clay, with a Piece of barke or leafe, some with a sear cloth of waxe and butter, which as they be not much needfull, so they hurt not, unlesse that by being busie about them, you move your graffs from their places. They use also mosse, tyed on above the clay with some bryar, wicker, or other bands. These profit nothing. They all put the graffes in danger, with pulling and thrusting : for I hold this generall rule in graffing and planting; if your stock and graffes take and thrive (for some will take and not thrive, being tainted by some meanes in the planting or graffing) they will (without doubt) recover their wounds safely and shortly.

General rule.

The best time of graffing from the time of removing your stock is the next Spring, for that saves a second wound, and a second repulse of sap, if your stock be of sufficient bignesse to take a graffe from as big as your thumbe, to as big as an arme of a man. You may graffe lesse (which I like)& bigger, which I like not so well. The best time of the year is in the last part of *Februarr* or *March*, or beginning of *Aprill*, when the Sun with his heat begins to make the sap stirre more rankly about the change of the moon, before you see any great apparency of leafe or flowers, but onely knots and buds, and before they be proud, though it be sooner : Cherries, Peares, Apricoks, Quinces, and Plummes would be gathered and grafted sooner.

Time of graffing.

The graffes may be gathered sooner in *February*, or any time within a month, or two before you graffe, or upon the same day (which I commend)If you get them any time before : for I

Gathering of graffes.

E

have

have knowne graffes gathered in *December* and doe well , take heed of drought I have my felf taken a burke not of a tree, and the fame day when he was laid in the earth about mid *February* gathered grafts and but in him , and one of thofe graffes bore **Graffes of old** the third yeare after, and the fourth plentifully ; Graffes of old **trees.** trees would be gathered fooner then of young trees for they fooner breake and bud. If you keepe graffes in the earth, moifture with the heat of the Sun wil make them fprout as faft, as if they were growing on the tree. And therefore feeing keeping is dangerous, the fureft way(as I judge)is to take them within a weeke of the time of your grafting.

    The grafts would be taken not of the proudeft twigs,for it may **Where taken.** be your ftock is not anfwerable in ftrength. And therfore(fay I) the grafts brought from South to us in the North although they take and thrive(which is fomewhat doubtfull, by reafon of the difference of the clime and carriage)yet fhall they in time fafhion themfelves to our cold Northern foile,in grouth,tafte,&c.

    Nor of the pooreft ;for want of ftrength may make them unready to receive fap (and who can tell but a poor graft is tainted)nor on the outfide of your tree , for there fhould your tree fpread, but in the middeft: for there you may be fure your tree is no whit hindered in his grouth or forme . He will ftil recover inward, more then you would wifh. If your clay clift in Summer with drought, looke well in the Chinkes for Emmets and Earwigs,for they are cunning and clofe theeves,about grafts ; **Emmits.** you fhall find them ftirring in the morning and evening and the rather in the moift weather . I have had many young buds of Graffs, even in the flourifhing, eaten with Ants. Let this fuffice for graffing,which is in the faculty counted the cheife fecret,and becaufe it is moft ufuall, it is beft knowne.

    Graffes are not to be difliked for grouth,till they wither,pine, and die. Ufually before *Midfummer* they break,if they live.Some (but few)keeping proud and green, will not put till the fecond yeer,fo is it to be thought of Sets.

    The firft fhew of putting is no fure figne of grouth,it is but the fap the graffe brought with him from his tree.

    So foone as you fee the graft put forth grouth , take away the clay, for then doth neither the ftock nor the graft need it,(put a
little

little frefh well tempered clay in the hole of the ftock,) for the clay is now tender, and rather keeps moifture then drought.

The other waies of changing the naturall fruit of Trees, are more curious then profitable and therefore I mind not to beftow much labour or time about them, onely I fhall make knowne what I have proved, and what I doe thinke.

And firft of incifing, which is the cutting of the back of the *Incifing.* boale, a rine or branch of a tree at fome bending or knee, fhoul-derwife with two gafhes, onely with a fharp knife to the wood: then take a wedge, the bignes of your graf, fharp ended, flat on the one fide, agreeing with the tree, and round on the other fide, and with that being thruft in, raife your bark, then put in your graffe, fafhioned like your wedge juft: and laftly cover your wound, and faft it up, and take heed of ftraining. This will grow but to fmall purpofe, for it is weak hold, and lightly it will be under grouth. Thus may you graft betwixt the bark and the *A great ftock.* tree of a great ftock that will not eafily be clifted But I have try-ed a better way for great trees, *viz.* Firft, cut him off ftraight, and cleanfe him with your knife, then cleave him into four quarters, equally with a ftrong cleaver: then take for every clift two or three fmall (but hard) wedges, juft of the bigneffe of your grafts, and with thofe wedges driven in with a hammer, open the four clifts fo wide (but no wider) that they may take your four graffes with thrufting, not with ftraining: and laftly cover and clay it clofely; and this is a fure & good way of grafting: or thus; clift your ftock by his edges twice or thrice with your clever, and open him with your wedge in every clift one by one, and put in your graffes and then cover them. This may doe well.

Packing on is when you cut aflope a twig of the fame bigneffe *Packing thus* with your graft, either in or befides the knot, two inches long, and make your graft agree jump with the cyon, and gafh your graft and your cyon in the middeft of the wound, length-way, a ftraw breadth deep, and thruft the one into the other, wound to wound, fap to fap, barke to barke, then tye them clofe and clay them. This may doe well. The faireft graft I have in my little Orchard, which I have planted, is thus packt on, and the branch whereon I put him, is in his plentifull roote.

To be fhort in this point, cut your graft in any fort or fafhion

E 2

two

two inches long and joyne him cleanly and close to any other
sprig of any tree in the latter end of the time of grafting, when
sap is somewhat rife, and in all probability they will close and
thrive · thus.

The sprig.   The graft.   The twig.   The graft.

Or any other fashion you thinke good.

Inoculating.

Inoculating is an eye or bud, taken bark and all from one
tree, and placed in the room of another eye or bud of another;
cut both of one compas, and their bound. This must be done
in Summer, when the sap is proud.

Much like unto this, is that they call grafting in the scutch-
ion, they differ thus: That here you must take an eye with his
leaf, or (in mine opinion) a bud with his leaves (Note that an

Grafting in
Scuthion.

eye is for a scion, a bud is for flowers and fruit) and place them
on an other tree, in a plain (for they so teach:) the place
or bark where you must set it, must bee thus cut with a
sharp knife, & the barke raised with a wedge, and then the
eye or bud put in & so bound up. I cannot deny but such may
grow. And your bud if he take will flower, and beare fruit in
that year: as some grafts and sets also, being set for
bloomes. If these two kindes thrive, they reforme but a spray
and an under grow.h. Thus you may place Roses or thornes,
and Cherries on Apples, and such like. Many write much more
of grafting, but to smal purpose. Whom we leave to themselves,
and their followers, and ending this secret, we come in the next
chapter to a point of knowledge most requisite in an Arborist
as well for all other woods as for an Orchard.

CHAP. II
Of the right dressing of Trees.

IF all these things aforesaid were indeed performed, as we
have shewed them in words, you should have a perfect orchard

Necessity of
dressing trees.

nature & substance, begun to your hand : And yet are all these
things nothing, if you want that skil. to keep and dresse your
trees. Such is the condition of all earthly things, whereby a
man receiveth profit or pleasure; that they degenerate presently

ly without good ordering. Man himſelf left to himſelfe, growes
from his heavenly and ſpirituall generation, and becometh
beaſtly yea deviliſh to his own kind, unleſſe he be regenerate.
No marvell then, if trees make their ſhoots, and put their ſprays
diſorderly. And truly (if I were worthy to judge) there is not a
miſchiefe that breedeth greater and more generall harme to all
the Orchard (eſpecially if they be of any continuance that ever I
ſaw, (I will not except three) then the want of the ſkilfull dreſſing of trees. It is a common and unſkilfull opinion, and ſaying,
Let all grow, and they will beare more fruite: and if thou lop a-
way ſuperfluous boughs they ſay what a pitty is this? how many
apples would theſe have borne? not conſidering there may ariſe Generall rule
hurt to your Orchard, aſwell (nay rather) by abundance as by
want of wood. Sound and thriving plants in a good ſoile will
ever yeeld too much wood, and diſorderly, but never too little.
So that a ſkilfull and painfull Arboriſt need never want matter
to effect a plentifull and well dreſt orchard: for it is an eaſie
matter to take away ſuperfluous boughs (if your gardiner have
skill to know them) whereof your plants will yeeld abundance,
and ſkill will leave ſufficient well ordered. All ages both by
rule and experience do conſent to a pruning and lopping of
trees: yet have not any that I know deſcribed unto us (except in
dark and generall words) what or which are thoſe ſuperfluous
boughes, which we muſt take away, and that is the chiefe and
moſt needfull point to be knowne in lopping. And we may well
aſſure our ſelves, (as in all other Arts, ſo in this) there is a vantage
and dexterity by ſkill, and an habite by practiſe out of experience, in the performance hereof for the profit of mankind; yet
doe not I know (let me ſpeak it with the patience of our cunning Arboriſts) any thing within the compaſſe of human affaires
ſo neceſſary, and ſo little regarded, not onely in Orchards,
but alſo in all other timber trees, where, or whatſoever.

How many forrests and woods wherein you ſhall have for one
lively thriving tree, foure (nay ſometimes twenty foure) evill Timber wood
evill dreſt.
thriving, rotten and dying trees, even while they live? and in
ſtead of trees, thouſands of buſhes and ſhrubs. What rottenneſſe?
what hollowneſſe? what dead armes? withered tops? curtalled
trunks? what loads of moſſes? drouping boughs? and dying

E 3 branch-

branches you shall see every where? And those that are like in this sort are in a manner all unprofitable boughs, cankered arms, crooked, little and short boals: what an infinite number of bushes, shrubs, and skrogs of hazels, thornes, and other profitable wood, which might be brought by dressing to become great and goodly trees? Consider now the cause: The lesser wood hath been

The cause of
hurts in woods

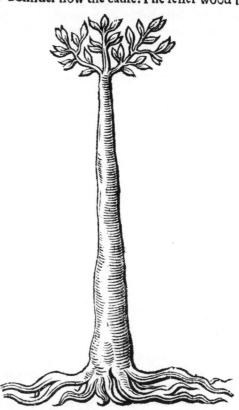

Imagin the root to be spread far wider.

spoyled with carelesse, unskilfull, and untimely stowing and much also of the great wood. The greater trees at the first rising have filled and over-laden themselves with a number of wastful boughs] boughes and fuckers, which have not only drawne the fap from the boale but alfo have made it knotty, and themfelves and the boale moffie for want of dreffing, whereas if in the prime of grouth they had beene taken away clofe, all but one top(accor- Dreffe timber ding to this pattern)and cleane by the bulke the ftrength of all trees how. the fap fhould have gone to the bulke, and fo he would have recovered and covered his knots,and have put forth a faire long and ftraight body(as you fee) for timber profitable, huge, great of bulke and of infinite laft

If all timber trees were fuch (will fome fay) how fhould we have crooked wood for whdels,&c?

Anfw. Dreffe all you can, and there will be enough crooked for thofe ufes.

More then this, in moft places, they grow fo thick, that nei- ther themfelves, nor earth, nor any thing under or neer them can thrive, nor Sun, nor rain, nor aire can doe them, nor any thing neere or under them, any profit or comfort

I fee a number of Hags, where, out of one roote you fhall fee three or foure (nay more, fuch is mens unskilfull greedineffe, who defiring many have none good) pretty Okes or Afhes ftraight and tall, becaufe the root at the firft fhoot gives fap a- maine: but if one onely of them might be fuffered to grow, and that well and cleanly pruned, all to his very top, what a tree fhould we have in time? And wee fee by thofe roots continually and plentifully fpringing,notwithftanding fo deadly wounded, what a comodity fhould arife to the owner, and the Common- wealth, if wood were cherifhed, and orderly dreffed.

The waft boughs clofely and skilfully taken away,would give Profit of trees us ftore of fences and fuell, and the bulk of the tree in time dreffed. would grow of huge length and bigneffe. But here(me thinkes) I heare an unskillfull Arborift fay, that trees have their feverall formes, even by nature, the Peare, the Holly, the Afpe, &c grow long in bulk with few and little armes, the Oke by nature broad and fuch like. All this I grant : but grant me alfo, that there is a profitable end and ufe of every tree, from which if it decline The end of (though by nature) yet man by art may (nay muft)correct it. trees. Now other end of trees I could never learne then good timber. fruit much and good ; and pleafure; ufes phyficall hinder no- thing a good forme. Nei-

Trees wil take any forme.

Neither let any man so much as thinke,that it is unprofitable much lesse unpossible, to reforme any tree of what kind soever For(beleeve me)I have tryed it, I can bring any tree(beginning betimes)to any forme The Peare and Holly may be made to spread,and the Oke to close.

But why doe I wander out of the compasse of mine Orchard into the Forrests and Woods? Neither yet am I from my purpose,if boals of timber-trees stand in need of all the sap,to make them great and streight (for strong grouth and dressing makes strong trees)then it must be profitable for fruit(a thing more immediatly serving a mans need) to have all the sap his root can yeeld: for as timber sound, great, and long, is the *good of timber trees,* and therefore they beare no fruite of worth: so fruit, good,

The end of trees.

sound,pleasant,great and much, is the end fruite trees. That gardiner therefore shall performe his dutie skilfully & faithfully, which shall so dresse his trees, that they may beare such and such store of fruit,which he shall never doe(I dare undertake)unlesse he keep this order in dressing his trees.

How to dresse a fruit-tree.

A fruit tree so standing, that there need none other end of dressing but fruite(not ornaments, not walks, nor delight to such as would please their eye only , and yet the best forme cannot but both adorne and delight)must be parted from within two foot or there abouts,of the earth,so high to give libertye to dresse his roote, and no higher , for drinking up the sap that should feed his fruit ,for the boale will be first , and best served and fed , because he's next the roote , and of greatest waxe and substance, and that makes him longest of life, into two,three or foure armes , as your stocke or graffes yeeld twigs , and every arme into two or more branches , and every branch into his severall syons, still spredding by equall degrees ,so that his lowest spray be hardly without the reach of a mans hand,and his highest be not past two yards higher, rarely(especially in the middest)that no one twig touch his fellow. Let him spread as farre as he lift without his maister-bough, or lop equally. And when any bough doth grow sadder and fall lower then his fellowes (as they will with weight of fruit)ease him the next spring of his superfluous twigs,and he will Rise when any bough or spray shall amount above the rest ; either snub his top with a nip betwixt

twixt your finger and your thumb, or with a sharpe knife, and take him cleane away, and so you may use any Cyon you would reforme; and as your tree growes in stature and strength, so let him rise with his tops but slowly, and early, especially in the middest, and equally, and in breadth also; and follow him upward with lopping his under grouth and water-boughes, keeping the same distance of two yards, but not above three in any wise, betwixt the lowest and the highest twigs.

1. Thus you shall have well-liking, cleane-skind, healthfull, great, and longlasting trees.

Benefits of good dressing.

2. Thus shall your tree grow low, and safe from winds, for his top will be great, broad, and weighty.

Remedy.

3. Thus growing broad, shall your trees beare much fruit (I dare say) one as much as sixe of your common trees and good without shadowing, dropping and fretting; for his boughes branches, and twigs shall be many, and those are they (not the boale) which beare fruite.

4. Thus shall your boale being little (not small, but low) by reason of his shortnesse, take little, and yeeld much sap to fruit.

5. Thus your trees by reason of strength in time of setting shall put forth more blossomes and more fruit, being free from taints (for strength is a great help to bring forth much) and safely, whereas weaknesse fails in setting, though the season be calme.

Some use to bare trees roots in winter, to stay the setting till hotter seasons, which I discommend, because

1. They hurt the roots.

2. It stayes nothing at all.

3. Though it did, being small, with us in the North they have their part of our *Aprill* and *May* Frosts.

4. Hinderance cannot profit weak trees in setting.

5. They wast much labour.

6. Thus shall your tree be easie to dresse, and without danger, either to the tree or the dresser.

7. Thus may you safely and easily gather your fruit without falling bruising, or breaking of Cyons.

This is the best forme of a fruit tree, which I have here shaddowed

F

dowed

meanes in time die : For the fap preffeth upward ; and it is like
dowed out for the better capacity of them that are led more
with the eye, then the mind, craving pardon for the deformity,
becaufe I am nothing skilfull either in the painting or carving.

Imagine that the paper makes but one fide of the tree to appeare, the whole round compaffe will give leave for many more
armes, boughes, branches, and cyons.

The perfect forme of a Fruit tree.

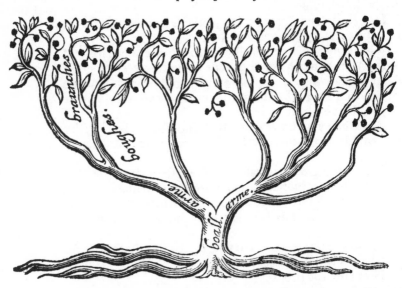

If any tree cannot well be brought to this forme : *Experto crede Roberto,* I can fhew divers of them under twenty years of age.
Time beft for   The fitteft time of the Moone for proyning, is, as of grafting,
proyning.   when the fap is ready to ftirre (not proudly ftirring) and fo to
cover the wound ; and of the yeere, a moneth before (or at leaft
when) you graffe. Dreffe Peares, Apricocks, Peaches, Cherries,
and Bullys fooner. And old trees before young plants, you may
dreffe at any time betwixt Leafe and Leafe. And note where you
take any thing away, the fap the next Summer will be putting :
Be fure therefore when he puts a bud in any place where you
would not have him, rub it off with your finger.   And

And here you muſt remember the common homely proverbe :
Dreſsing be-
          Soone crookes the tree.   time.
          That good Camrell muſt be.

Begin betimes with trees, and do what you liſt : but if you let
them grow great and ſtubborne, you muſt doe as the tree liſt.
They will not bend but break, nor be wound without danger.
A ſmall branch will become a bough, and a bough an arme in
bigneſſe. Then if you cut him, his wound will feſter, and hardly
without good skill recover: therefore, *Obſta principiis.* Of ſuch   Faults of eviſt
wounds and leſſer, or any bough cut off a handfull or more from   dreſt trees and
the body, comes hollowneſſe, and untimely death. And there-   the remedy.
fore when you cut, ſtrike cloſe, and cleane, and upward, and leave
no bunch.

This forme in ſome caſes ſometimes may be altered : If your
tree, or trees, ſtand neere your Walkes, if it pleaſe your fancy   The forme al-
more, let him not break till his boal be above your head : ſo may   tereth.
you walk under your trees at your pleaſure. Or if you ſet your
fruit trees for your ſhades in your Groves, then I reſpect not the
forme of the tree but the comlineſſe of the walke.

All this hitherto ſpoken of dreſsing, muſt be underſtood of   Dreſsing of old
young plants, to be formed : it is meet, ſomewhat be ſaid for the   trees.
inſtruction of them that have old trees already formed, or rather
deformed : for *Malum non vitatur niſi cognitum.* The faults
therefore of a diſordered tree, I find to be five.
    1. An unprofitable boale.
    2. Water boughes.   Faults are five,
    3. Fretters.   and their re-
    4. Suckers. And,   medies.
    5. One principall top.
A long boale asketh much feeding, and the more he hath the
more he deſires, and gets, (as a drunken man drink, or a covetous   Long boale.
man wealth,) and the leſſe remaines for the fruit ; he puts his
boughes into the ayr, and makes them, the fruit and it ſelfe more   No remedy.
dangered with winds : for this I know no remedy, after that the
tree is come to grouth ; once evill, never good.

Water boughes, or under grouth, are ſuch boughes as grow
low under others, and are by them over grown, overſhadowed,   1 Water
dropped on, and pinde for want of plenty of ſap, and by that   boughes.
                    F 2   meane

water in her courſe, where it findeth moſt iſſue, thither it floweth leavi ng the other leſſe ſluices dry even as wealth to wealth, and much to more. Theſe ſo long as they beare, they beare leſſe, worſe and fewer fruit, and wateriſh.

Remedy.

The remedy is eaſie, if they be not grown greater then your arme, lop them cloſe and cleane, and cover the middle of the wound; the next Summer when he is dry, with a ſalve made of tallow, tarre and a very little pitch, good for the covering of any ſuch wound of a great tree: unleſſe it be bark-pild, and then

Bark-pild, and the remedy.

a ſeare cloth of freſh butter, hony and waxe preſently (while the wound is green) applyed, is a ſoveraigne remedy, in Summer eſpecially. Some bind ſuch wounds with a thumb rope of hay, moiſt, and rub it with dung.

Fretters.

Fretters are, when as by the negligence of the Gardner, two or more parts of the tree, or of diverſe trees, as armes, boughes branches, or twigs, grow ſo neere and cloſe together, that one

Touching.

of them by rubbing doth wound one another. This fault of all other ſhewes the want of skill (or care at leaſt) in the arboriſt: for

Remedy.

here the hurt is apparent, and the remedy eaſie, ſeene to, betimes: galls are wounds incurable, but by taking away thoſe members: for let them grow, and they will be worſe and worſe, and ſo kill themſelves with civill ſtrive for roomth, and danger the whole tree. Avoid them betime therefore, as a common wealth doth boſome enemies.

Suckers.

A Sucker is a long, proud, and diſorderly Cyon, growing ſtreight up (for pride of ſap makes proud, long, and ſtreight grouth) out of any lower parts of the tree receiving a great part of the ſap, and bearing no fruit, till it have tyranized over the whole tree. Theſe are like idle and great Drones amongſt Bees: and proud and idle members in a common wealth.

The remedy of this is, as of water boughes, unleſſe they be growne greater then all the reſt of the bonghes; and then your Gardner (at your diſcretion) may leave him for his boale, and take away all, or the moſt of the reſt. If he by little ſlip him, and ſet him, perhaps he will take: my faireſt Apple tree was ſuch a ſlip.

One principal top or bough, and remedy.

One or two principall top-boughes are as evill, in a manner as ſuckers; they riſe of the ſame cauſe, and receive the ſame remedy:

medy: yet thefe are more tolerable, becaufe thefe beare fruit, yea
the beft:but Suckers of long time do not beare.

I know not how your tree fhould be faulty, if you reforme Inftruments for dreffing.
all your vices timely, & orderly. As thefe rules ferve for dreffing
young trees, and fets in the firft fetting : fo may they well ferve
to help old trees, though not exactly to care them.

The inftruments fitteft for all thefe purpofes, are moft commonly, for the greateft trees, an handfome, long, light Ladder
of Firpoles, a little, nimble, and ftrong armed Saw, and fharpe.
For leffe trees, a little and fharp Hatchet, a broad mouthed
Chefell, ftrong and fharp, with an hand-beetle, your ftrong and
fharp Clever, with a knock, and (which is a moft neceffary inftru-
ment amongft little trees) a great hafted & fharp knife or whit-
tle. And as needfull is a ftool on the top of a Ladder of eight or
more rungs, with two back feet, whereon you may fafely, and eafily ftand to graffe, to dreffe, and to gather fruit,
thus formed. The feet may be faft wedged in : but
the Ladder muft hang loofe with two bands of I-
ron. And thus much of dreffing trees for fruit, for-
mally to profit.

CHAP. 12.
Of Soyling.

THere is one thing yet very neceffary for to make your Or- Neceffity of
chard both better, and more lafting : Yea fo neceffary, that foiling.
without it your orchard cannot laft, nor profper long, which
is neglected generally both in precepts and in practife, *viz.* manuring with Soil: whereby it happeneth that when trees (amongft
other evils) through want of fatneffe to feed them, become moffie, and in their grouth are evill (or not thriving) it is either at-
tributed to fome wrong caufe, as age (when indeed they are but Trees great
young) or evill ftanding (ftand they never fo well) or fuch like, Suckers.
or elfe the caufe is altogether unknowne, and fo not amended.

Can there be devifed any way by nature, or art, fooner or
foundlier to fuck out, and take away the heart of earth, then by
great trees ; fuch great bodies cannot be fuftained without great
ftore of fap ? What living body have you greater then of trees ?
The great Sea monfters (whereof one came a land at *Teefemouth*

F 3 in

in *Yorkeshire*, hard by us, 18 yards in length, and neere as much in compasse)seeme hideous,huge,strange,and monstrous, because they be indeed great, but especially, because they are seldome seene::but a tree liking, comne to his grouth and age, twice that length, and of a bulke never so great, besides his other parts,is not admired,because he is so commonly seen. And doubt not, but if he were well regarded from his kernell, by succeeding ages, to his full strength, the most of them would double their meafure.About fifty yeeres ago, I heard by credible and constant reports, That in *Brookham* Park in *Westmer land,* neer unto *Penrith,* there lay a blowne Oake, whose trunk was so bigge that two Horsemen being the one on the one side, and the other on the other side, they could not see one another : to which if you ad his arms,boughs,& roots, & confider of his bigneffe,what would he have been,if preserved to the vantage?Also I read in the history of the *West-Indians*, out of *Peter Martyr,* that fixteen men taking hands one with another, were not able to fathome one of those trees about. Now nature having given to such, a faculty by large and infinite roots, taws and tangles , to draw immediatly his suftenance from our common mother the earth(which is like in this point to al other mothers that bear) hath also ordained that the tree over-loden with fruit, and wanting sap to feed all she hath brought forth, will waine all she cannot feed, like women bringing forth more children at once then she hath teats. See you not how trees especially,by kind being great, standing so thick and close , that they cannot get plenty of sap, pine away all the graffe, weeds, leffer shrubs and trees ; yea, and themselves also, for want of vigour of fap?so that trees growing large,sucking the soyl whereon they stand continually and amaine, and the foizon of the earth that feeds them decaying (for what is there that wasts continually, that shall not have an end?)must either have supply of sucking, or else leave thriving and growing. Some grounds will beare corn while they be new,and no longer, because their cruft is shallow, and not very good, and lying they scind and wash and become barren. The ordinary corne soyls continue not fertile, without following & soyling,& the best requires supply even for the little body of corne. How then can we think that any

ny

ny ground how good foever can fuftaine bodies of fuch great-
neffe, and fuch great feeding, without great plenty of fap arifing Great bodies.
from good earth ? This is one of the chiefe caufes why fo many
of our Orchards in England are fo evill thriving when they
come to grouth, and our fruit fo bad. Men are loth to beftow
much ground, and defire much fruit, and will neither fet their
trees in fufficient compaffe, nor yet feed them with manure.
Therefore of neceffity Orchards muft be foiled.

The fitteft time is, when your trees are growne great, and
have neer hand fpread your Earth, wanting new earth to fuftain
them, which if they doe, they will feek abroad for better earth :
and fhun that which is barren (if they find better) as catrel evill
pafturing. For nature hath taught every creature to defire and
feeke his owne good, and to avoid hurt. The beft time of the
yeare is at the fall, that the froft may bite and make it tender, and
the raine wafh it into the roots . The Summer time is perilous
if ye dig, becaufe the fap ftirs amain. The beft kind of foyl is
fuch as is fat, hot, and tender. Your earth muft be lightly opened, that the Dung may go in, and wafh away ; and but fhallow,
left you hurt the roots : and in the fpring, clofely and equally
made plain againe for fear of Suckers. I could wifh, that after my
trees have fully poffeffed the foyle of mine Orchard, that every
feven yeers at leaft, the foil were befpread with Dung halfe a foot
thick at leaft. Puddle water out of the dunghill poured on plentifully, will not onely moiften but fatten efpecially in *June* and
July. If it be thick and fat, and applyed every yeere, your Orchard fhall need none other foiling. Your ground may lye fo low
at the River fide, that the flood ftanding fome dayes and nights
thereon, fhall fave you all this labour of foiling.

CHAP. 13.
Of Annoyances.

A Chiefe help to make every thing good, is to avoid the e-
vills thereof : you fhall never attain to that good of your
Orchard you look for, unlefs you have a gardner that can difcerne the Difeafes of your trees, and other annoyances of your
Orchard, and find out the caufes thereof, and know and apply
fit remedies for the fame. *For be your ground fuch plants and trees*
as you would wifh, if they be wafted with hurtfull things, what

have

have you gained, but your labour for your travell ? It is with an Orchard and every Tree, as with mans body. The best parts of physick for preservation of health, is to foresee and cure diseases.

Two kinds of evills in an Orchard. All the diseases of an Orchard are of two sorts, either internall, or externall. I call those inwards hurts which breed on, and in, particular trees.

1 Galles.	5 Bark bound.
2 Canker.	6 Bark pild.
3 Mosse.	7 Worme.
4 Weaknesse in setting.	8 Deadly wounds.

Galls. Galls, Cankers, Mosse, Weaknesse, though they be divers diseases, yet (howsoever authors think otherwise) they rise all out of the same cause.

Galls we have described with their cause and remedy, in the 11 Chapter under the name of fretters.

Canker. Canker is the consumption of any parts of the tree bark and wood; which also in the same place is deciphered under the title of water-boughes.

Mosse. Mosse is sensible seen and knowne of all, the cause is pointed out in the same chapter, in the discourse of timber-wood, and partly also the remedy: but for Mosse adde this, that any time in summer (the spring is best, when the cause is removed) with an Hair cloth immediatly after a showre of raine, rub off your mos or with a piece of wood (if the mosse abound) formed like a great knife.

Weaknesse in setting. Weaknesse in the setting of your fruit shall you find there also in the same chapter, and his remedy. All these flow from the want of roomth in good soile, wrong planting, Chapter. 7. and evill, or no dressing.

Bark-bound. Bark-bound as I think riseth of the same cause, and the best and present remedy (the causes being taken away) is with your sharp knife in the spring, length-way to lance his barke thorow-out 3 or 4 sides of his boul.

Worme. The disease called the worm is thus discerned : the bark will be hollow in diverse places like gall, the wood will dye & dry, and you shall see easily the bark swell : it is verily to be thought that therein is bred some worme. I have not yet thorowly sought it out, because I was never troubled therewithall : but only

onely have seen such trees in divers places. I thinke it a worme rather,because I see this disease in trees, bringing fruit of sweet tast,and the swelling shewes as much. The remedy(as I conjecture)is, so soon as you perceive the wound, the next Spring cut it out bark and all, and apply Cows pisse and vinegar presently, and so twice or thrice a week for a moneths space : For I well perceive, if you suffer it any time, it eates the tree or bough round,and so kills. *Since I first wrote this treatise, I have changed my mind concerning the disease called the worme, because I read in the history of the West-Indians, that their trees are not troubled with the disease called the Worm or Canker, which ariseth of a raw and evill concocted humor or sap. Witnesse* **Pliny** : *by reason the Country is more hot then ours ; wherefore I think the best remedy is (not disallowing the former, considering that the Worme may breed by such an humor) warme standing, sound lopping, and good dressing.*

Bark-pilld you shall finde with his remedy, in the eleventh Chapter.

Deadly wounds are,when a mans *Arborist* wanting skill,cuts off armes,boughes or branches an inch; or (as I see sometimes) an handfull, or halfe a foot or more from the body : *these so cut, cannot cover in any time with sap,and therefore they dye, and dying they perish the heart, and so the tree becomes hollow, and with such a deadly wound cannot live long.* Wounds. Remedy.

The remedy is,if you find him before he be perished,cut him close, as in the 11. Chapter : if he be hoal'd, cut him close, fill his wounds though never so deep, with morter well tempered, & so,close at the top his wound with a Sear-cloth nailed on,that no ayr nor rain approach his wound. If he be very old and declining, he will recover; and the hole being closed, his wound within shall not hurt him for many years.

Hurts on your trees are chiefly Ants, Earwigs, and Caterpillars.Of Ants and Earwigs is said Chap.10. *Let there be no swarm of pis-mires neer your tree roots,no not in your Orchard : turne them over in a frost,and poar in water,and you kill them.*

For *Caterpillers,* the vigilant Fruiterer shall soone espy their lodging by their web, or the decay of leaves eaten round about them. And being seen,they are easily destroyed with your hand,

G or

or rather (if your tree may fpare it) take fprig and all: for the red fpeckled Butter-fly doth ever put them, being her fperm, among the tender fprays for better feeding; efpecially in drought: & tread them under your feet. I like nothing of fmoak among trees. Unnaturall heats are nothing good for naturall trees. *This, for Difeafes of particular trees.*

Externall hurts are either things naturall, or artificiall. Naturall things externally hurting Orchards.

I Beafts.	I Deer.	II Birds.	I Bulfinch.
	2 Goats.		2 Thrufh.
	3 Sheep.		3 Blackbird.
	4 Hare.		4 Crowe.
	5 Cony.		5 Pye,
	6 Cattell.		&c:
	7 Horfe.		

The other things are.
1 Winds.
2 Cold.
3 Trees.
4 VVeeds.
5 VVormes.
6 Moles.
7 Filth.
8 Poyfonfull fmoke.

Externall wilfull evills are thefe.
1 Walls.
2 Trenches.
3 Other workes noifome, done in or neere your
4 Evill Neighbours.   (Orchard.
5 A careleffe Mafter.
6 An undifcreet, negligent, or no keeper.

See you here an whole army of mifcheifes banded in troops againft the moft fruitfull trees the earth beares? affailing your good labours. Good things have moft enemies.

Remedy.   A skilfull Fruiterer muft put to his helping hand, and difband and put them to flight.

Deere. &c-   For the firft rank of beafts, befides your out ftrong fence, you muft have a faire and fwift Grey-hound, a Stone-bow, Gun, and

if

if need require, an Apple with an hook for a Deer, and an hare-pipe for an Hare.

Your Cherries, and other Berries, when they be ripe, will _{Birds.} draw all the Black-birds, Thrushes, and Mag-pies, to your Orchard. The Bull finch is a devourer of your fruit in the bud, I have had whole trees shal'd out with them in winter time.

The best remedy here is a Stone-Bow, a Piece, especially if you have a musket, or sparrow-hawke in winter to make the Black-bird stoop into a bush or hedge.

The gardner must cleanse his soile of all other trees, but fruit trees, as aforesaid, *chap.2.* for which it is ordained ; & I would e-specially name Oaks, Elms, Ashes, and such other great wood, but that I doubt it should be taken as an admission of lesser trees for I admit of nothing to grow in my Orchard but fruit and flowers : if sap can hardly be good to feed our fruit trees, should we allow of any other ? especially those that will become their Masters, and wrong them in their lively hood.

And although we admit without the fence, of wall-nuts in most plain places, Trees middle most, and Ashes or Oaks, or Elms ut-most, set in comely rowes equally distant, with fair Allyes twixt row and row, to avoid the boisterous blasts of winds, and within them also others for bees, yet we admit none of these into your Orchard plat : other remedies then this have we none against the nipping frost.

Weeds in fertile soil (because the generall course is so) till _{Weeds.} your trees grow great, will be noisome, and deforme your allies walks, beds, and squares ; your under-gardeners must labour to keep all cleanly and handsome from them, and all other filth, with a spade, weeding knives, rake with Iron teeth, a scraple of I-ron thus formed,

For Nettles, and ground Ivy after a shower.

When weeds, straw, sticks, and all other scrapings are gathered together, burn them not, but bury them under your crust in any place of your Ochard, and they will dye & fatten your ground.

G 2

Wormes

V Vormes.
Moles.

Wormes and Moales open the earth, and let in ayre to the roots of your trees, and deforme your squares and walks; and feeding in the earth, being in number infinite, draw on barrennesse.

Remedy.

Wormes may easily be destroyed. Any Summer evening when it is darke, after a showre with a candle you may fill bushels, but you must tread nimbly, and where you cannot come to catch them so sift the earth with coal-ashes an inch or two thicknesse, and that is a plague to them, so is sharp gravell.

Moales will anger you, if your gardner or some other moalcatcher ease you not ; especially having made their fortresses among the roots of your trees ; you must watch her well with a Moal-speare, at morning noone and night : when you see her utmost hill, cast a trench betwixt her and her home (for shee hath a principall mansion to dwell and breed in about *April*, which you may discerne by a principall hill, wherein you may catch her, if you trench it round and sure, and watch well ; or wheresoever you can discern a single passage (for such she hath) there trench, and watch, and have her.

Wilfull annoyances must be prevented and avoided by the love of the Maister and Fruiterer, which they bear to their Orchard.

Justice and liberality will put away evill neighbours, or evill neighbour-hood. And then (if God blesse and give successe to your labours) I see not what hurt your Orchard can sustaine.

CHAP. XIIII.
The age of Trees.

IT is to be considered, All this treatise of trees tends to this end, that men may love and plant Orchards, whereunto there cannot be a betrer inducement then that they know (or at least be perswaded) that all the benefit they shall reap thereby, whether of pleasure or profit, shall not be for a day, or a moneth, or one, or many, but many hundred years. Of good things the greatest, and most durable is alwayes the best. If therefore out of reason grounded upon experience, it be made (I think) manifest, but I am sure probable, that a fruit tree in such a soyle
and

and fite, as is defcribed, fo planted and trimmed and kept as is a-
fore appointed, and duely foiled, fhall dure a thoufand yeers,
why fhould we not take pains, and be at two or three yeers char-
ges (for under feven years will an Orchard be perfected for the
firft planting, and in that time be brought to fruit)to reap fuch
a commodity, and fo long lafting? *The age of trees.*

Let no man think this to be ftrange, but perufe and confider
the reafon. I have apple trees ftanding in my little Orchard,
which I have known thefe fourty yeers, whofe age before my
time I cannot learne, it is beyond memory, though I have inqui-
red of divers aged men of 80 years and upwards : thefe trees although come into my poffeffion very ill ordered, and mifhapen,
and one of them wounded to his heart, and that deadly, (for I
know it will be his death)with a wound, wherein I might have
put my foote into the heart of his bulke, (now it is leffe) not-
withftanding, with that fmall regard they have had fince, they
fo like, that I affure my felfe they are not come to their grouth
by more then two parts of three, which I difcerne not onely by
their own grouth, but alfo by comparing them with the bulk of
other trees. And I find them fhort (at leaft) by fo many parts in
bigneffe, although I know thofe other fruit trees to have been
much hindred in their ftature by evill guiding. Herehene I gather
thus. *Gathered by reafon out of experience.*

If my trees be a hundred yeeres old, and yet want two hundred of their grouth before they leave increafing, which make
three hundred, then muft we needs refolve, that this three hundred yeers are but the third part of a trees life ; becaufe (as all
things living befides)fo trees muft have allowed them for their
increafe one third, another third for their ftand, and a third
part of time alfo for their decay. All which time of a tree a-
mounts to nine hundred yeers; three hundred for increafe, three
hundred for his ftand, whereof we have the terme [ftature] and
three hundred for his decay : and yet I thinke (tor we muft conjecture by comparing, becaufe no one man liveth to fee the full
age of trees) I am within the compaffe of his age, fuppofing alwaies the forefaid meanes of preferving his life. Confider the
age of other living creatures. The Horfe and moiled Oxe,
wrought to an untimely death, yet double the time of their in- *Parts of a trees age.*

increafe. A dog likewife increafeth three, ftands three at leaft, and in as many (or rather more) decayes.

Every living thing beftowes the leaft part of his age in his growth and fo muft it needs be with trees. A man comes not to his full growth and ftrength (by common eftimation) before thirty yeers and fome flender and clean bodies, not till forty: fo long alfo ftands his ftrength, and fo long alfo muft he have allowed by courfe of nature to decay. Ever fuppofing that he be well kept with neceffaries and from and without ftraines, bruifes and all other dominiering difeafes. I will not fay upon true report, that Phyfick holds it poffible, that a clean body kept by thefe three Doctors, *Doctor Dyet, Doctor Quiet,* and *Doctor Merryman,* may live neer a hundred years. Neither will I here urge the long yeares of *Methufelah,* and thofe men of that time, becaufe you will fay, Mans dayes are fhortned fince the flood. But what hath fhortned them? God for mans fins; but, by meanes: as want of knowledge, evill government, riot, gluttony, drunkenneffe, and (to be fhort) the encreafe of the curfe, our fins increafing in an Iron and wicked age.

Now if a man, whofe body is nothing (in a manner) but tender rottenneffe, whofe courfe of life cannot by any meanes, by counfell, reftraint of Lawes or punifhment, nor hope of praife profit or eternall glory, be kept within any bounds, who is degenerate clean from his natural feeding, to effeminate nicenefs, and cloying his body with excefs of meat, drink, fleep &c. and to whom nothing is fo pleafant and fo much defired, as the caufes of his own death, as idlenefs, luft, &c. may live to that age: I fee not but a tree of a folid fubftance, not damnified by heat or cold, capable of, and fubject to any kind of ordering or dreffing that a man fhall apply unto him, feeding naturally, as from the beginning, difburdened of all fuperfluities, eafed of, and of his owne accord avoiding, the caufes that may annoy him, fhould double the life of a man, more then twice told : and yet natural Philofophy, and the univerfal confent of all Hiftories tell us, that many other living creatures far exceed man in length of yeares: As the Hart, and the Raven. Thus reporteth that famous *Roterdam* out of *Hefiodus,* and many other Hiftoriographers. The teftimony of *Cicero* in his book *De Senectute,* is weighty to this

this purpose:that we muſt *in poſteras ætates ſerere arbores,* which can have none other ſenſe, but, that our fruit trees whereof he ſpeakes,can indure for many ages.

What elſe are trees,in compariſon with the earth,but as haires to the body of a man ? And it is certain, without poyſoning, evill and diſtemperate dyet, and uſage, or other ſuch forcible cauſe,the haires dure with the body. That they be called excrements,it is by reaſon of their ſuperfluous growth : (for cut them as often as you liſt, and they will ſtill come to their naturall length)Not in reſpeƈt of their ſubſtance, and nature. Haires endure long, and are an ornament, and of uſe alſo to the body, as trees to the earth.

So that I reſolve upon good reaſon, that fruit trees well ordered, may live and like a thouſand yeares, and beare fruit;and the longer, the more, the greater, and the better, becauſe his vigour is proud and ſtronger,when his yeeres are many.You ſhal ſee old trees put forth their buds and bloſſomes both ſooner and more plentifull then young trees, by much. And I ſenſibly perceive my young trees to inlarge their fruit as they grow greater, both for number and greatneſſe. Young Heifers bring not forth Calves ſo fair, neither are they ſo plentifull to milke ,as when they become to be old Kine. No good Houſ-wife will breed of a young but of an old breed-mother:It is ſo in all things naturally,therefore in trees.

And if fruit trees laſt to this age, how many ages is it to be ſuppoſed, ſtrong and huge timber trees will laſt ? whoſe huge The age of Timber trees. bodies require the yeares of divers *Methuſelaes,* before they end their dayes, whoſe ſap is ſtrong and bitter, whoſe barke is hard and thicke,and their ſubſtance ſolid and ſtiffe:all which, are defences of health and long life. Their ſtrength withſtands all forciple winds, their ſap of that quality is not ſubjeƈt to wormes and tainting. Their bark receives ſeldome or never by caſualty any wound.And not onely ſo,but he is free from removals,which are the death of millions of trees, whereas the fruit-tree in compariſon, is little and often blown down,his ſap ſweet; eaſily, and ſoon tainted,his bark tender, and ſoon wounded, and himſelf uſed by man,as man uſeth himſelf, that is,either unskilfully or careleſſely.

It

Age of trees difcerned. It is good for fome purpofes to regard the age of your fruit trees which you may eafily know, till they come to accomplifh twenty yeeres, by his knots: Reckon from his root upward an arme, and fo to his toptwig, and every years grouth is diftinguifhed from other by a knot, except lopping or removing doe hinder.

CHAP. XV.
Of gathering and keeping Fruit.

Generall rule. ALthough it be an eafie matter, when God fhall fend it, to gather and keep fruit, yet are there certaine things worthy your regard. You muft gather your fruit when it is ripe, and not before, elfe will it wither, and be tough and fower. All fruits generally are ripe, when they begin to fall. For trees doe as all other bearers doe, when their young ones are ripe, they will wain them. The Dove her Pigeons, The Coney her Rabbets, and women their Children. Some fruit-trees fometimes getting a taint in the fetting with a froft or evill wind, will caft his fruit untimely, but not before he leave giving them fap, or they leave growing. Except from this forefaid rule, Cherries, Damfons & Bullyes. The Cherry is ripe when he is fwelled, wholly red, and fweet. Damfons and bullies not before the firft froft.

Cherries, &c.

Apples. Apples are knowne to be ripe, partly by their colour growing towards a yellow, except the Leather-coate, and fome Peares, and greenings.

When. Timely Summer fruit will be ready, fome at midfummer moft at Lammas for prefent ufe; but generally no keeping fruit before *Michael tide.* Hard winter fruit, and Wardens longer.

Gather at the full of the Moone for keeping, gather dry for feare of rotting.

Dry ftalkes. Gather the ftalks withall: for a little wound in fruit is deadly but not the ftump, that muft bear the next fruit; nor leaves, for moifture putrifies.

Severally. Gather every kind feverally by it felfe, for all will not keep alike and it is hard to difcerne them, when they are mingled

Over laden trees. If your trees be over laden (as they will be, being ordered, as is before taught) I like better of pulling fome off (though they be

be not ripe) neer the top end of the bough, then of propping
by much, the reft fhall be better fed. Propping puts the boughs in
danger, and frets it at leaft.

Inftruments : A long ladder of leight firre, a ftool-ladder as Inftruments.
in the eleventh chapter. A gathering-apron like a poake before
you, made of purpofe, or a Wallet hung on a bough, or a baf-
ket with a fieve bottome, or skin bottome, with lathes or fplin- Bruifes.
ters under, hung in a rope to pull up and downe : bruife none,
every bruife is to fruit, death: if you doe, ufe them prefently: an
hooke to pull boughes to you is neceffary, break no boughes.

For keeping, lay them in a dry loft, the longeft keeping Ap Keeping.
ples firft and furtheft on dry ftraw, on heaps, ten or fourteene
dayes, thicke, that they may fweat. Then dry them with a foft
and cleane cloth, and lay them thin abroad. Long keeping fruit
would be turned once in a month foftly but not in, nor immediatly after froft. In a loft, cover'd well with ftraw, but rather
with chaffe or branne: For froft doth caufe tender rottenneffe.

CHAP. XVI.
Of profits:

NOw paufe with your felfe, and view the end of all your labours in an Orchard : unfpeakable pleafure, and infinite
commodity. The pleafure of an Orchard I refer to the laft chapter, for the conclufion;& in this chapter, a word or two of the
profit, which thorowly to declare is paft my skill :& I account it
as if a man fhould attempt to adde light to the Sun with a candle, or number the ftarres. No man that hath but a mean Orchard or judgment but knowes, that the commodity of an Orchard is great : Neither would I fpeak of this, being a thing fo
manifeft to all;but that I fee, that through the carelefnefs of men,
it is a thing generally neglected. But let them know, that they
lofe hereby the chiefeft good which belongs to houfe keeping.

Compare the commodity that commeth of halfe an acre of
ground, fet with fruite-trees and he arbs, fo as is prefcribed, and
an whole acre (fay it be two) with corn, or the beft commodity
you can wifh and the orchard fhall exceed by divers degrees.

In *France* and fome other countries, and in *England*, they Cyder and
make great ufe of Cider and Perry, thus made: dreffe every Perry.
apple, the ftalke, upper end, and all galls away, ftamp them, and
H   ftraine

ftraine them, and within twenty four howers tun them up into clean, fweet, and found veffels, for fear of evill ayre, which they will readily take : and if you hang a poakefull of Cloves, Mace, Nutmegs, Cinamon, Ginger, and pils of Lemons in the middeft of the veffell, it will make it as wholefome & pleafant as wine. The like ufage doth Perry require.

Thefe drinks are very wholefome; they coole, purge, and prevent hot agues. But I leave this skill to Phyfitians.

Fruit. The benefit of your Fruit, Roots, and Herbs, though it were but to eat and fell, is much.

Waters. Waters diftilled of Rofes, Woodbind, Angelica, are both profitable and wondrous pleafant, and comfortable. Saffron and Licoras will yeeld you much.

Cconferves, and preferves, are ornaments to your feafts, health in your Sickneffe, and a good help to your freind, and to your

Conferves. purfe.

He that will not be moved, with fuch unfpeakable profits, is well worthy to want, when others abound in plenty of good things.

C H A P. XVII.

Ornaments.

Me thinkes hitherto we have but a bare Orchard for fruit, and but halfe good, fo long as it wants thofe comely Ornaments that fhould give beauty to all our labours, and make much for the honeft delight of the owner and his friends.

Delight the chiefe end of Orchards. For it is not to be doubted, but as God hath given man things profitable, fo hath he allowed him honeft comfort, delight, and recreation in all the works of his hands. Nay, all his labours under the Sun without this are troubles, and vexations of mind : For what is greedy gaine, without delight, but moyling, and turmoiling in flavery? But comfortable delight, with content, is the good of every thing, and the pattern of heaven. A morfell of bread with comfort, is better by much then a fat Oxe with unquietneffe. And who can deny but the Principall

An Orchard delightfome. end of an Orchard, is the honeft delight of one wearied with the workes of his lawfull calling? The very works of, and in an Orchard and Garden, are better then the eafe and reft of, and from other labours. When God had made man after his owne
Image,

Image, in a Perfeſt ſtate, and would have him to repreſent himſelfe in authority, tranquillity, and pleaſure upon the earth, he placed him in *Paradiſe*. What was *Paradiſe*? but a Garden and Orchard of trees and hearbs, full of pleaſure? and nothing there but delights. The gods of the earth reſembling the great God of heaven in authority, Maieſty and abundance of all things, wherein is their moſt delight? and whither do they withdraw themſelves from the troubleſome affairs of their eſtate, being tyred with the hearing and judging of litigious controverſies, choaken (as it were) with the cloſe ayre of their ſumptuous buildings, their ſtomacks cloyed with variety of Banquets their ears filled and overburthened with tedious diſcourſings? whither? but into their Orchards? made and prepared, dreſſed and deſtinated for that purpoſe, to renew and refreſh their ſenſes, and to call home their over-wearied ſpirits. Nay, it is (no doubt) a comfort to them, to ſet open their caſements into a moſt delicate Garden and Orchard, whereby they may not onely ſee that, wherein they are ſo much delighted, but alſo to give freſh, ſweet and pleaſant aire to their Galleries and chambers.

    And look what theſe men do by reaſon of their greatneſſe and ability, provoked with delight, the ſame doubtleſſe would every of us doe, if power were anſwerable to our deſires : whereby we ſhew manifeſtly, that of all other delights on earth, they that are taken by Orchards are moſt excellent and moſt agreeing with nature.

    For whereas every other pleaſure commonly fills ſome one of our ſenſes, and that onely, with delight; this makes all our ſenſes ſwim in pleaſure, and that with infinite variety, joyned with no leſſe commodity.

    That famous *Philoſopher*, and matchleſſe Oratour, *M.T.C.* preſcribeth nothing more fit, to take away the tediouſneſſe of old age. three or foureſcore yeers, then the pleaſure of an Orchard.

    What can your eye deſire to ſee, your ears to heare, your mouth to taſt, or your noſe to ſmell, that is not to be had in an Orchard, with abundance of variety? What more delightſome then an infinite variety of ſweet ſmelling flowers? decking with ſundry colours, the green mantle of the earth, the univerſall

Side notes:
An Orchard in Paradice.

Cauſe of weariſomneſſe.

Orchard is the remidie.

All delight in Orchards.

This delights all the ſenſes.

Delighteth old age.

Cauſes of delight in any Orchard.

mother of us all, so by them bespotted, so dyed, that all the world cannot sample them, and wherein it *is* more fit to admire the dyer, then imitate his workmanship, colouring not onely the earth, but decking the aire, and sweetning every breath and spirit.

Flowres.

The Rose red, damask, velvet, and double double province Rose, the sweet musk Rose double and single, the double and single white Rose; The faire and sweet senting woodbine, double and single, and double double. Purple Cowslip, and double Cowslips, and double double Cowslips; Primrose double and single. The Violet nothing behind the best, for smelling sweetly. A thousand more will provoke your content.

Borders and squares.

And all these by the skill of your Gardner, so comelily and orderly placed in your borders & squares; and so intermingled, that one looking thereon cannot but wonder, to see, what nature corrected by Art, can doe.

Mounts.

Whence you may shoot a Buck.
Dial.
Musick.

When you behold in diverse corners of your Orchard *Mounts* of stone or wood, curiously wrought within and without, or of earth covered with fruit trees, Kentish Cherries, damsons, Plums, &c. with staires of precious workmanship; and in some corner (or moe) a true diall or clock, and some Antickworks and especially silver-sounding Musick, mixt instruments, and voyces, gracing all the rest: How will you be wrapt with Delight?

Walks.

Seats.

Large Walks, broad and long, close and open, like the *Tempe*-groves in *Thessaly*, raised with gravell and sand, having seats and banks of Cammomile; all this delights the mind, and brings health to the body.

Order of trees.

View now with delight the works of your owne hands, your fruit-trees of all sorts, loaden with sweet blossomes, and fruit of all tastes, operations and colours: your trees standing in comely order which way soever you look.

Shape of men and beasts.

Your borders on every side hanging and drooping with Feberries, Raspberries, Barberries. Currans; and the roots of your trees powdred with Strawberries, red, white and green, what a pleasure is this? Your Gardner can frame your lesser wood to the shape of men armed in the field, ready to give battell: of swift running Greyhounds, or of well sented and true running

Hounds

Hounds to chafe the Deer,or hunt the Hare. This kind of hunting
fhall not waft your corne; nor much, your coyne.

Mazes well framed a mans height, may perhaps make your Mazes.
friend wander in gathering of berries till he cannot recover
himfelf without your help.

To have occafion to exercife within your Orchard : it fhall be Bowling-Al-
a pleafure to have a bowling Alley, or rather (which is more ley.
manly, and more healthfull) a paire of Buts,to ftretch your Buts.
arms.

Rofemary and fweet Eglantine are feemly ornaments about Herbes.
a Doore or Window,and fo is Woodbine.

Look Chapt 15 and you fhall fee the forme of a Conduit. If Conduit.
there were two or more,it were not amifs.

And in mine owne opinion I could highly commend your
Orchard, if either through it, or hard by it, there fhould runne
a pleafant River with filver ftreams:you might fit in your River.
Mount, and angle a peckled Trout,fleighty Eel, or fome other
dainty Fifh Or moats, whereon you might row with a Boat and Moats.
fifh with Nets.

Store of Bees in a dry and warm Bee-houfe, comely made of Bees.
Fir boards to fing, and fit, and feed upon your flowers and
fprouts, make a pleafant noyfe and fight. For cleanly and innocent Bees, of all other things, love and become, and thrive in an
Orchard. If they thrive(as they muft needs, if your Gardner be
skilfull,and love them for they love their friends,and hate none
but their enemies)they will befides the pleafure,yield great profit to pay him his wages. Yea,the increafe of twenty Stocks or
Stooles,with other fees,will keep your Orchard

You need not doubt their ftings, for they hurt not whom
they know,and they know their keeper and acquaintance. If you
like not to come among them, you need not doubt them: for
but neat their ftore, and in their owne defence, they will not
fight,and in that cafe onely(and who can blame them ?)they are
manly, and fight defperately. Some (as that honourable Lady
at *Hacknes*, Whofe name doth much grace mine Orchard,ufe
to make feats for them in the ftone walls of their Orchard, or
Garden,which is good,but wood is better.

A Vine overfhadowing a feat, is very comely, though her Vine.
Grapes with us ripen flowly.   One

One chiefe grace that adornes an Orchard, I cannot let flip : a brood of Nightingales, who with feverall notes and tunes, with a ſtrong delightſome voyce out of a weak body, will bear you company night and day. She loves (and lives in)hots of woods in her heart She will help you to cleanſe your trees of Caterpillers, and all noyſome wormes and flies. The gentle Robin-red-breſt will help her,& in winter in the coldeſt ſtorms will keep a part. Neither will the filly Wren be behind in Summer, with her diſtinct whiſtle, (like a ſweet Recorder)to cheare your ſpirits

The Black-bird and Threſtle (for I take it, the Thruſh fings not,but devours)fing loudly in a *May* morning,and delights the eare much,and you need not want their company , if you have ripe Cherries or Berries, and would as gladly as the reſt doe your pleaſure : but I had rather want their company than my fruit

What ſhall I ſay? A thouſand of pleaſant delights are attending an Orchard : and ſooner ſhall I be weary then I can reckon the leaſt part of that pleaſure which one that hath,and loves an Orchard, may find therein.

What is there of all theſe few that I have reckoned , which doth not pleaſure the eye, the eare , the ſmell, and taſt? And by theſe ſenſes as Organs, Pipes , and windows, theſe delights are carried to refreſh the gentle, generous, and noble mind.

To conclude , what joy may you have, that you living to ſuch an age, ſhall ſee the beſſings of God on your labours while you live, and leave behind you to heirs , or ſucceſſors(for God will make heirs)ſuch a work, that many ages after your death , ſhall record your love to their Countrie? And the rather, when you conſider(*Chap.* 14.) to what length of time your worke is to laſt.

Birds-
Nightingale.

Robin-red-
breſt.
Wren.

Black-bird.
Thruſh.

Your owne
labour.

FINIS.

THE
COUNTRY HOVSE-WIVES
GARDEN,

Containing Rules for herbs, and Seeds,
of common ufe, with their times and feafons
when to fet and fow them.

Together
With the Husbandry of Bees, publifhed
with fecrets very neceffary for every *Houf-*
wife : as alfo divers new Knots for Gardens.

The Contents fee at large, in the laft Page.

Genef. 2. 29.

I have given unto you every Herb, and every tree, that fhall be to
you for meat.

LONDON,
Printed by *W. Wilfon,* for *E. Brewfter,* and *George*
Sawbridge, at the Bible on Ludgate-hill,
neere Fleet bridge. 1656.

THE COUNTRY
HOVSWIFES
GARDEN.

CHAP. I.

The Soyle.

He Soyl of an Orchard and Garden, differ
only in thefe three poynts : Firft, the Gar-
dens foil would be fomewhat dryer, becaufe   Dry.
herbs being more tender then trees, can neither abid moyfture nor drought, in fuch
exceffive meafure, as trees ; and therefore
having a dryer foyl, the remedy is eafie a-
gainft drought, if need be : water foundly ;
which may be done with fmall labour the compaffe of a Gardꞔn
being nothing fo great, as of an Orchard : and this is the caufe
(if they know it that Gardners raife their fquares : but if moyfture trꞔuble you, I fee no remedy without a generall danger,   HꞔPs.
except in Hopps, which delight much in a low and fappy
earth.

Secondly, the foyl of a Garden would be plaine and levell, at
leaft every fquare (for we purpofe the fquare to be the fitteft
form) the reafon is the earth of a garden wanting fuch helps, as
fhould ftay the water, which an orchard hath, & the roots of herbs
I   being

ing mellow and loofe, is foon either wafht away, or fends out his heart by too much drenching and wafhing.

Thirdly, if a garden foil be not cleere of weeds, and namely of grafs, the herbs fhall never thrive : for how fhould good herbs profper, when evill weeds wax fo faft: confidering good herbs are tender in refpeẻt of evill weeds : thefe being ftrengthened by nature, and the other by art ? Gardens have fmall place in comparifon, and therefore may more eafily be followed, at the leaft one half year before, and the better dreffed after it is framed. And you fhall find that clean keeping doth not only avoid danger of gathering weeds, but alfo is a fpeciall ornament, and leaves more plentifully fap for your tender herbs.

CHAP. II.
Of the Sites.

I Cannot fee in any fort, how the fite of the one fhould not be good, and fit for the other : The ends of both being one, good, wholefome, and much fruit joyned with delight, unleffe trees be more able to abide the nipping frofts than tender herbs : but I am fure, the flowers of trees are as foon perifhed with cold: as any herbe except Pumpion, and Melons.

CHAP. III.
Of the Forme.

L Et that which is faid in the Orchards forme, fuffice for a garden in generall : but for fpeciall formes in fquares, they are as many, as there are devices in Gardners braines. Neither is the wit and art of a skilfull Gardner in this point not to be commended, that can worke more variety for breeding of more delightfome choice, and of all thofe things, where the owner is able and defirous to be fatisfied. The number of formes, Mazes and Knots is fo great, and men are fo diverfly delighted, that I leave every Houfe-wife to her felf, efpecially feeing to fet downe many, had been but to fill much paper ; yet leaft I deprive her of all delight and direẻtion, let her view thefe few, choife, new formes; and note this generally, that all plots are fquare, and all are bordered about with Privit, Raifins, Fea-berries, Rofes, Thorne, Rofemary, Bee-flowers, Ifop, Sage, or such like.

CHAP.

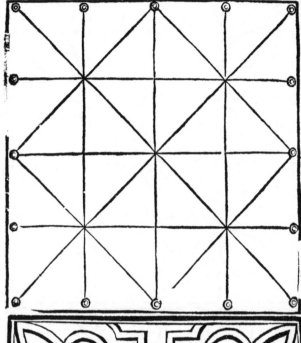

The ground
plot for knots.

Cinkfoile.

Flower
deluce.

The Tre-

The Fret.

Lozenges.

Crossebow.

Diamond.

Ovall.

Maze.

CHAP. IIII.
Of the Quantity.

A Garden requireth not so large a scope of ground as an Orchard, both in regard of the much weeding, dressing and removing, and also the pains in a Garden is not so well repayed home, as in an Orchard : It is to be granted, that the Kitchin garden doth yeeld rich gains, by berries, roots, cabbages, &c. yet these are no way comparable to the fruit- of a rich Orchard: But notwithstanding I am of opinion that it were better for *England* that we had more Orchards and Gardens, and more large. And therefore we leave the quantity to every mans ability and will.

CHAP. V.
Of Fence.

SEeing we allow Gardens in Orchard-plots, and the benefit of a Garden is much, they both require a strong and shrowding fence. Therefore leaving this, let us come to the Herbs themselves, which must be the fruit of all these labours.

CHAP. VI.
Of two Gardens.

HErbes are of two sort, and therefore it is meete(they requiring diverse manners of Husbandry)that we have two Gadens : A garden for flowres and a Kitchin garden:or a Summer garden:not that we mean so perfect a distinction, that wee meane the Garden for flowrs should or can be without herbs good for the Kitchin,or the Kitchin garden should want flowres, nor on the contrary : but for themost part they would be severed : first because your Garden flowers shall suffer some disgrace,if among them you intermingle Onions,Parsnips,&c. Secondly,your Garden that is durable, must be of one form : but that which is your Kitchens use, must yeelddaily roots, or other herbs and suffer deformity. Thirdly, the herbs of both will not be both alike ready, at one time, either for gathering, or removing. First therefore.

Of

Of the Summer Garden.

THefe hearbs and flowrs are comely and durable for fquares &
Knots, and all to be fet at *Michaeltide*, or fomewhat before;
that they may be fetled in, and taken with the ground before
winter; though they may be Set, efpecially fown, in the fpring.

Rofes of all forts (fpoken of in the Orchard) muft be Set.
Some ufe to Set flips and twine them, which fometimes, but feldome, thrive all.

Rofemary, Lavender, Bee-flowres, Ifop, Sage, Time, Cowflips,
Pyony, Daifies, Clove Gilliflowres, Pinks, Sothernwood, Lillies,
of all which hereafter.

Of the Kitchin Garden.

THough your Garden for flowres doth in a fort peculiarly
challenge to it felf a perfit, and exquifite form to the eyes,
yet you may not altogether neglect this, where your herbs for
the pot do grow. And therefore fome here make comely borders
with the hearbs aforefaid. The rather becaufe abundance of
Rofes and Lavender, yeeld much profit, & comfort to the fences :
Rofe water Lavender, the one cordiall (as alfo the Violets, Burrage, and Buglas) the other reviving the fpirits by the fence of
fmelling: both moft durable for fmell, both in flowres and water: you need not here raife your beds, as in the other garden,
becaufe Summer towards, will not let too much wet annoy
you. And thefe hearbs require more moyfture: yet muft you have
your beds devided, that you may go betwixt to weed, and fomewhat of form would be expected : To which it availeth that you
place your herbs of biggeft growth, by walles , or in borders, as
Fennell, &c. and the loweft in the middeft, as Saffron, Strawberries, Onions, &c.

CHAP. VII.
Divifion of Herbs:

GArden herbs are innumerable, yet thefe are common, and
fufficient for our Country-houfwives.

Herbs of greateft growth.
       K   Fen-

Fennell, Angelica, Tanſie, Hollihock, Lovage, Elicampane, French Mallowes, Lilies, French Poppie, Endive, Succory, and Clary.

Herbs of middle growth.

Burrage, Bugloſſe, Parſly, Sweet Sicily, Flower-deluce, Stock, gilliflowres, Wall-flowers, Anniſeeds, Coriander, Fether-few Mary-goldſ, Oculus Chriſti, Langdibeef, Alexanders, Carduus-benedictus.

Herbs of ſmalleſt growth.

Panſie, or Harts-eaſe, Coaſt-Marjoram, Savory, Strawberries, Saffron, Lycoras Daffadowndillies, Leeks, Chives, Chibbals, Skerots Onions, Batchelors buttons, Daſies, Peniroyal.

Hitherto I have only reckoned up and put in this rank, ſome Herbs: their Husbandry followes, each in an Alphabetical order, the better to be found.

CHAP. VIII.
Husbandry of Hearbs.

ALexanders: are to be renewed as Angelica. It is a timely Potherb.

Angelica is renewed with the ſeed, whereof he beareth plenty the ſecond year and ſo dyeth. You may remove the roots the firſt year. The leaves diſtilled, yeild water ſoveraign to expel paine from the ſtomack. The roote dryed taken in the fall, ſtoppeth the pores againſt infections.

Anniſeeds make their growth, and bear ſeeds the firſt yeere and dieth as Coriander: it is good for opening the pipes, and it is uſed in Comfits.

Artichoakes: are renewed by dividing the roots into Sets, in *March*, every third or fourth year. They require a ſeverall uſage, and therefore a ſeverall whole plot by themſelves, eſpecially conſidering they are plentifull of fruit much deſired.

Burrage and Bugleſſe: two Cordials renew themſelves by ſeed yearely, which is hard to be gathered, they are exceeding good Pot-herbs, good for Bees, and moſt comfortable for the heart and ſtomack, as *Quinces* and Wardens.

Camomile: ſet roots in banks and walks. It is ſweet ſmelling, qualifying head-ach.

Cab-

Cabbages: require great roome, they ſeed the ſecond year, ſow them in *February*, remove them when the plants are an handfull long, ſet deep and wet. Look well in drought for the white Caterpillars worme, the ſpaunes under the leaf cloſely: for every living Creature doth ſeek food and quiet ſhelter, and growing quick they draw to, and eat the heart : you may find them in a rainy dewy morning.

It is a good Pot-hearbe, and of this hearb called *Cole*, our Country Houſewifes give their pottage their name, and call them *Caell*.

Carduus Benedictus, or bleſſed : thiſtle ſeeds and dyes the firſt year, the excellent vertue thereof I referre to Herballs, for we are Gardiners, not Phyſicians.

Carrets are ſown late in *Aprill* or *May*, as Turneps, elſe they ſeed the firſt year, & then their roots are naught: the ſecond yeere they dye, their roots grow great and require large roome.

Chibals or Chives have their roots parted, as Garlick, Lillies. &c. and ſo are they ſet every third or fourth year : a good pot-hearb, opening, but evill for the eyes.

Clary is ſowne, it ſeeds the ſecond year, and dyes. It is ſomewhat harſh in taſt, a little in pottage is good, it ſtrengtheneth the reines.

Coaſt, Root parted, makes Sets in *March* : it beares the ſecond year: it is uſed in Ale in *May*.

Coriander is for uſage and uſes, much like Anniſeeds.

Daffadowndillies: have their roots parted & ſet once in three or four year or longer time. They flower timely, and after *Midſummer* are ſcarcely ſeen. They are more for Ornament, then for uſe, ſo are Daiſies.

Daiſie roots, parted and Set, as Flowre deluce and Camomile, when you ſee them grow too thicke or decay. They be good to keep up, and ſtrengthen the edges of your borders, as Pinks, they be red, white, mixt.

Ellicampane root is long laſting, as is the Lovage it ſeeds yearely, you may divide the roote, and ſet the root; taken in winter it is good (being dryed, powdered and drunk) to kill itches.

Endive and Succory are much like in nature, ſhape, and uſe, they

K 2

they renew themselves by seed, as Fennell, and other herbs. You
may remove them before they put forth shanks: a good Pot-
herbe.

Fennell is renewed, either by the seeds (which it beareth the
second yeer, and so yeerly in great abundance (sown in the fall or
Spring; or by deviding one root into many Sets, as Artichoke.
It is long of growth & life. You may remove the root unshankt:
It is exceeding good for the eyes, distilled, or any other wise taken: it is used in dressing Hives for swarmes; a very good Pot-
hearb, or for Sallets.

Fetherfew shakes seed. Good against a shaking Fever, taken
in a posset drink fasting.

Flower deluce, long lasting, Divide his roots, and Set: the roots
dryed have a sweet smell.

Garlick may be Set an handfull distance, two inches deep, in
the edge of your beds. Part the head into severall cloves, and e-
very clove, set in the latter end of *February*, will increase to a
great head before *September*: good for opening, evill for eyes:
when the blade is long, fast two & two together, the heads will be
bigger.

Hollihock riseth high, seedeth and dyeth, the chief use I know
is ornament.

Isop is reasonable long lasting: young roots are good Set,
slips better. A good pot-hearbe.

July-flowres, commonly called Gilly-flowres, or Clove July-
flowres (I call them so, because they flowre in July) they have the
name of Cloves, of their sent. I may well call them the King of
flowres except the Rose) & the best sort of the are called *Queen*-
July flowres. I have of them nine or ten severall colours, & divers
of them as big as Roses; of all flowres (save the Damaske Rose)
they are the most pleasant to sight and smel: they last not past
three or four yeers unremoved. Take the slips (without shanks)
and Set any time save in extreame frost, but especially at *Michael-tide.* Their use is much in ornament, and comforting the spirits, by the sense of smelling.

July flowres of the wall, or wall-July-flowres, Wall-flowres
or Bee-flowres, or Winter-July-flowres, because growing in the
walls even in winter, and good for Bees, will grow even in stone-
walls

walls,they will feem dead in Summer, and yet revive in Winter
they yeeld feed plentifully, which you may fow at any time,
or in any broken earth, efpecially on the top of a mud-wall,
but moift, you may fet the root before it be brancht, every flip
that is not flowr'd will take root ; or crop him in Summer, and
he will flowre in winter, but his winter feed is untimely. This
and Palmes are exceeding good, and timely for Bees.

Leeks yeeld feed the fecond year,unremoved;and dye, unlefs
you remove them,ufually to eat with Salt and Bread,as Onyons
alwayes green,good pot-herb,evill for the eyes.

Lavender-Spike would be removed within feven yeeres, or
eight at the moft : flips twined, as Hyfope and Sage, would take
beft at *Michael-tide.*This flowre is good for Bees, moft comfortable for fmelling, except Rofes:and kept dry, is as ftrong after a yeere,as when it is gathered. The water of this is comfortable.

White *Lavender* would be removed fooner.

Lettice yeelds feed the firft year,and dyes : fow betime ; and
if you would have them Cabbage for fallets, remove them as
you doe Cabbage.They are ufuall in Sallets and in the pot.

Lillies white and red, remove once in three or foure years
their roots yeeld many Sets,like the Garlicke. *Michael-tide* is
the beft. They grow high, after they get root. Thefe roots are
good to break a byle as are Mallows and Sorrel.

Mallowes, French or gagged, the firft or fecond yeer, feed
plentifully. Sow in *March,* or before. They are good for the
houfewifes pot, or to break a bunch.

*Marigolds,*moft commonly come of feed, you may remove
the Plants when they be two inches long.The double Marigold,
being as bigge as a little Rofe,is good for fhew.They are a good
Pot-hearb.

Oculus Chrifti, or Chrifts-eye, feedes and dyes the firft or fecond year :you may remove the young Plants, but feed is better.
One of thefe feeds put into the eye, within three or four houres
will gather a thick skinne, cleere the eye, and bolt it felfe forth
without hurt to the eye.A good Pot-hearbe,

Onyons are fown in *February,* they are gathered at *Michael-
tide,*and all the Summer long, for Sallet ; as alfo young parfly,

K 3   Sage

Sage, Chibals, Lettice, ſweet Sicily, Fennell, &c. good alone, or with meate, as muttons, &c. for ſawce eſpecially for the pot.

Parſly ſow the firſt yeer, and uſe the next yeer : it ſeeds plentifully; an hearb of much uſe, as ſweet ſicily is. The ſeed and roots are good againſt the ſtone.

Parſneps require an whole plot, they be plentiful and common; ſow them in *February*, the kings (that is in the middle) ſeed broadeſt and reddeſt. Parſneps are ſuſtenance for a ſtrong ſtomacke, not good for evill eies : VVhen they cover the earth, in a drought to tread the tops, makes the roots bigger.

Penny-royall, or pudding graſſe, creeps along the ground, like ground Ivie. It laſts long, like daiſies, becauſe it puts and ſpreads dayly new roots. Divide, and remove the roots, it hath a pleaſant taſt and ſmel, good for the pot, or hacktmeat, or Haggas pudding.

Pumpions : Set Seeds with your finger, a finger deep, late in *March*, and ſo ſoone as they appear, every night if you doubt froſt, cover them, and water them continually out of a water pot: they be very tender, their fruit is great and wateriſh.

French Poppy beareth a great flowre, and the ſeed will make you ſleep.

Raddiſh is ſauce for cloyed ſtomacks, as Capers, Olives and Cucumbers : caſt the ſeeds all ſummer long here and there, and you ſhall have them alwaies young and freſh.

Roſemary, the grace of hearbs here in England, in other Countries common. To ſet ſlips immediately after *Lammas*, is the ſureſt way. Seed ſown may prove well, ſo they be ſowne in hot weather, ſomewhat moyſt, and good earth : for the hearb, though great, is neſh and tender (as I take it) brought from hot Countries to us in the cold North: ſet thin, it becomes a window well. The uſe is much in meats, more in Phyſick, moſt for Bees.

Rue, or *hearb of grace*, continually greene, the ſlips are ſet. It laſts long as Roſemary, Sothernwood, &c. too ſtrong for mine Houſewifes pot, unleſſe ſhe will brew Ale therewith, againſt the plague: let them not ſeed if you will have him laſt

Saffron, every third yeere his roots would be removed at *Midſummer*, for when all other hearbs grow moſt, it dyeth. It flowreth at *Michael-tide*, and groweth all winter : keep his flowers from birds in the morning, and gather the yellow (for
they

they shape much like Lillies)dry,and after dry them: they be pretious, expelling diseases from the heart and stomack.

Savery· seeds and dyes the first year, good for my Housewifes pot and pye.

Sage: let slips in *May,* and they grow aye ; let it not seed, it will last the longer. The use is much and common. The Monkish proverb is *tritum.*

Cur moritur homo,cui salvia crescit in horto ?

Skerots: the roots are set when they be parted, as *Pionie,* and Flower deluce at *Michael-tide,* the root is but small and very sweet. I know none other speciall use but the Table.

Sweet *Sicely:* long lasting, pleasantly tasting, either the seed sowne, or the root parted, and removed, makes increase, it is of like use with parsley.

Strawberries : long lasting, set roots at *Michael-tide,* or the Spring, they be red, white, and greene, and ripe, when they be great and soft, some by *Midsummer with us.* The use is, they will coole my Housewife well, if they be put in wine or Creame with Sugar.

Time: both seeds, slips and roots are good, if it seed not, it will last three or four years or more, it smelleth comfortably. It hath much use namely, in all cold meats, it is good for Bees.

Turnep : is sown. In the second year they bear plenty of seed ; they require the same time of sowing that Carrets doe ; they are sick of the same disease that Cabbages be. The root increaseth much, it is most wholesome, if it be sowne in a good and well tempered earth; Soveraigne for eyes and bees.

I reckon these hearbs onely, because I teach my Country Housewife, not skilfull artists ; and it should be an endlesse labour, and would make the matter tedious to reckon up *Land-theefe, Stock-July-flowers, Charvell, Valerian, Go-to bed at noone, Piony, Lycoras, Tansie, Garden mints, Germander, Centaury,* and a thousand such Physick hearbs. Let her first grow cunning in this, and then she may inlarge her Garden as her skill and ability increaseth. And to help her the more, I have set downe these observations.

CHAP.

CHAP. IX.

General Rules in Gardening.

IN the South parts, Gardening may be more timely, and more safely done, then with us in *Yorkeshire*, because our ayr is not so favorable, nor our ground so good.

2 Secondly most seeds shakt, by turning the good earth, are renewed, their mother the earth keeping them in her bowels, till the Sun their Father can reach them with his heat.

3 In setting herbs, leave no top more then an handfull above the ground, nor more then a foote under the earth.

4 Twine the rootes of those slips you set, if they will abide it. Gilly flowres are too tender.

5 Set moist, and sowe dry.

6 Set slips without shanks at any time, except at *Midsummer*, and in frosts.

7 Seeding spoyles the most roots, as drawing the heart and sap from the root.

8 Gather for the pot and medicines, herbs tender and green the sap being in the top but in Winter the roote is best.

9 All the herbs in the Garden for flowres would once in seven years be renewed, or soundly watered with puddle water, except Rosemary.

10 In all your Gardens and Orchards, banks and Seats of Cammomile, Penny-royall, Daisies and Violets, are seemly and comfortable.

11 These require whole plots, Artichokes, Cabbages, Turneps Parsneps, Onyons, Carrets, and (if you will) Saffron and Skerrits.

12 Gather all your seeds, dead, ripe, and dry.

13 Lay not dung to the roots of your herbs, as usually they do: for dung not melted is too hot even for trees.

14 Thin setting and sowing (so the roots stand not past a foot distance) is profitable, for the herbs will like the better. Greater herbs would have more distance.

1 Set and sow herbs in their time of grouth (except at *Midsummer*

ſum ner, for then they are too too tender)but trees in their time of reſt.

16 A good houſewife may, and will gather ſtore of herbs for the pot, about Lammas, and dry them, and pound them, and in winter they will do good ſervice.

Thus have I limmed out a Garden to our Countrey Houſe-wives, and given them rules for common herbs. If any of them (as ſometimes they are) be knotty, I refer them to *Chap. 3.* The skill and pains of weeding the Garden with weeding knives of fingers, I refer to themſelves & their maids, willing them to take the opportunity after a ſhower of rain : withall, I adviſe the Miſ-treſſe either to be preſent her ſelf, or to teach her maids to know herbs from weeds.

CHAP. X.

The Huſbandry of Bees.

THere remaineth one neceſſary thing to be preſcribed, which in mine opinion makes as much for ornament as either flowers, or forme, or cleanneſſe, and I am ſure as commodious as any of, or all the reſt : which is Bees, well ordered. And I will not account her any of my good Houſe-wives, that want-eth either Bees, or skilfulneſſe about them. And though I know ſome have written well and truly, and others more plentifully upon this theme : yet ſomewhat have I learned by experience (being a Bee-maſter my ſelf) which hitherto I cannot find put into writing, for which I thinke our Houſe-Wives will count themſelves beholding unto mee.

The firſt thing that a Gardner about Bees muſt be carefull for, is an houſe not ſtakes and ſtones abroad, *Sub dio*: for ſtakes rot and reele, Raine and Weather eate your hives and covers, and cold moſt of all is hurtfull for your Bees. Therefore you muſt have an houſe made along a ſure dry wall in your Garden, neere, or in your Orchard for Bees love flowers and wood with their hearts.

Bee houſes.

L   This

This the form; a Frame ftanding on pofts with one floor (if
you would have it hold more Hives, two floores) boorded, layd
on bearers, and back pofts, covered over with boords, flat-wife.
Let the floores be without holes or clifts, left in cafting time

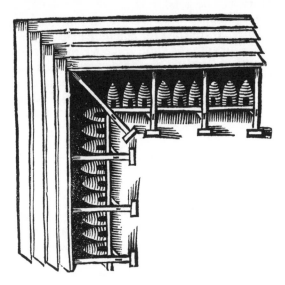

the Bees lye out and loyter.

And though your hives ftand within an handbredth the one
of another, yet will Bees know their home.

In this Frame may your Bees ftand dry and warme, efpecially
if you make dores like dores of windows to fhroud them in
winter, as in an houfe: provided you leave the hives mouth open.
I my felfe have devifed fuch an houfe, and I find that it ftrength-
ens my Bees much, and my hives will laft fix to one.

Hives.   M. *Markham* commends hives of wood ; I difcommend them
not : but ftraw-hives are in ufe with us, and I think, with all
the world , which I commend for nimbleneffe, clofeneffe,
warmneffe , and dryneffe. Bees love no externall motions of
daubing, or fuch like. Sometimes occafion fhall be offered to
lift and turn hives, as fhall appear hereafter. One light entire
                                                          hive

hive of ftraw, in that cafe, is better then one that is daubed, weighty and cumberfome. I wifh every hive, for a keeping fwarme, to hold three pecks at leaft in meafure. For too little hives procure Bees, in cafting time, either to ly out, and loyter, or elfe to caft before they be ripe and ftrong, and fo make weake fwarmes and untimely: Whereas if they have roome fufficient, they ripen timely, and cafting feafonably, are ftrong, and fit for labour prefently. Neither would the hive be too great, for then they loyter, and waft meat and time:

Your Bees delight in wood, for feeding, efpecially for cafting therefore want not an Orchard. A *May's* fwarme is worth a Mares Foale: if they want wood, they be in danger of flying away. Any time before *Midfummer* is good for cafting, and timely; before *July* is not evill. I much like M. *Markhams* opinion for having a fwarm in combs of a dead or forfaken hive, fo they be frefh and cleanly. To thinke that a fwarme of your own, or others, will of it felfe come into any fuch hive, is a meer conceit, *Experto crede Roberto*. His fmearing with hony, is to no purpofe, for the other bees will eat it up. If your fwarme knit in the top of a tree, as they will, if the wind beat them not to fall down, let the ftool or ladder prefcribed in the Orchard do you fervice. _{Hiving of Bees.}

The lefs your Spelkes are, the leffe is the waft of your Hony, and the more eafily will they draw, when you take your Bees. Four Spelkes a thwart, and one top Spelk are fufficient. The Bees will faften their combes to the Hive. A little Hony is good, but if you want, Fennel will ferve to rub your Hive withall. The Hive being dreft and ready fpelkt, rub'd and the hole made for their paffage (I ufe no hole in the Hive but a piece of woo i hoal'd, to fave the Hive and keep out Mice) fhake in your Bees, or the moft of them (for all commonly you cannot get) the remainder will follow. Many ufe fmoke, nettles, &c. which I utterly diflike: for Bees love not to be molefted. Ringing in the time of cafting is a meer fancy, violent handling of them is fimply evill, becaufe bees of all other creatures love cleanlinefs and peace. Therefore handle them leafurely and quietly, and their Keeper whom they know may do with them what he will without hurt: Being hived at night, bring them to their feat. Set your hives all of one year together. _{Spelks.}

Signes of breeding,if they be ſtrong.

1 They will avoid dead young Bees and Droans.

2 They will fweat in the morning,till it run from them , allwayes when they be ftrong.

Signes of caſting.

1 They will fly Droans by reafon of heat.

2 The young Swarme will once or twice in fome faire feafon come forth muftering, as though tney would caft,to prove themfelves,and go in again.

3 The night before they caft, if you lay your ear to the Hives mouth,you fhall hear two or three, but efpecially one above the reft,cry,Up,up,up, or Tout,tout,tout, like a Trumpet founding the alarum to the battel.

Much defcanting there is of, and about the Mafter Bee , and their degrees,order,and Government: but the truth in this point is rather imagined, then demonftrated·There are fome conjectures of it, *viz.* wee fee in the combs diverfe greater houfes then the reft,and we commonly bear the night before they caft,fometimes one Bee,fometimes two or more Bees,give a lowd and feverall found from the reft,and fometimes Bees of greater bodies then the common fort : but what of all this? I leane not on conjectures , but love to fet down that I know to be true , and leave thefe things to them that love to divine.

Keep none weak,for it is hazard oftentimes with lofs.Feeding will not help them; for being weak,they cannot come down to meat, or if they come down,they dye,becaufe Bees weak cannot abide cold. If none of thefe,yet will the other Bees being ftrong, fmell the honey,& come and fpoil & kill them. Some help is in cafting Time,to put two weak fwarms together,or as Tr. *Markham* wel faith,Let them not caft late, by raifing them with wood or ftone but with impes(fay I.)An impe is, three or four wreaths wrought as the Hive,the fame compafs,to raife the Hive withall but by experience in tryall I have found out a better way by Cluftering, for late or weake fwarmes; hitherto not found out of any that I know. That is this; After cafting time,if I have any ftock proud,and hindred from timely cafting,with former Winters poverty,or evill weather in cafting time, with two handles and crooks fitted for the purpofe,I turne up that ftock fo peftered

Catching.

Cluftering.

ftered with Bees,and fet it on the crown, upon which fo turned with the mouth upward I place another empty hive well dreft, and fpelkt, into which without any labour, the Swarme that would not depart,and caft,will prefently afcend,becaufe the old Bees have this quality (as all other breeding creatures have)to expell the young,when they have brought them up.

There will the Swarme build as kindly, as if they had of themfelves been caft. But be fure you lay betwixt the Hives fome ftraight and cleanly fticke or fticks , or rather a board with holes,to keep them afunder:otherwife they wil joyn their works together fo faft that they cannot be parted. If you fo keep them afunder at *Michael-tide*, if you like the weight of your fwarme (for the goodnefs of fwarms is tryed by the weight) fo catched, you may fet it by for a ftocke to keep Take heed in any cafe the combes be not broken, for then the other bees will fmell the honey, and fpoyl them. This have I tryed to be very profitable for the faving of bees.

The Inftrumet hath this form The great ftreight piece of wood,

the reft are irõ clafps &nails,the clafps are loofe in the ftaple;two men with two of thefe faftned to the Hive will eafily turn it up

They gather not till *July*; for then they be difcharged of their young,or elfe they are become now ftrong to labour & now fap in flowers is ftrong and proud by reafon of time, & force of Sun. And now alfo in the North (and not before)the hearbs of greateft vigour put forth their flowers;as Beans,Fennell,Burrage,&c.

The moft fenfible weather for them, is heat and drought,becaufe the nefh Bee can neither abide cold or wet : and fhowres (which they well fore fee)do interrupt their labours , unlefs they fall in the night, and fo they further them.

After cafting *Time*, you fhall benefit your ftocks much,if you help them to kill their Droans, which by all probability and judgement,are an idle kind of bees, and waftfull. Some fay they breed,and have feen young Droans in taking their honey,which I know is true. But I am of opinion that there are alfo Bees — Droanes.

L 3   which

which have loſt their ſtings, and ſo being as it were gelded, become idle and great : there is great uſe of them. *Deus & natura nihil fecit fuſtra.* They hate the bees, *and cauſe them caſt the ſooner:* they never come forth, *but when they be over heated: they never come home loaden* After caſting time, and when the bees want meat, *you ſhall ſee the labouring Bees faſten on them, two, three or four at once, as if they were theeves to be led to the Gallowes, and killing them, they caſt them out, and draw them far from home, as hatefull enemies.* Our Houſe-wife, if ſhe be the Keeper of her own bees(as ſhe had need to be) may with her bare hand in the heat of the day ſafely deſtroy them in the hives mouth. Some uſe towards night, in a hot day, to ſet before the mouth of the Hive a thin board with little holes in it, at which the leſſer Bees may enter, but not the Droans ; ſo that you may kill them at your pleaſure.

Snails ſpoil them by night like theeves: they come ſo quietly, and are ſo faſt, that the Bees fear them not: look early and late, eſpecially in a rainy or dewey evening or morning.

Mice are no leſſe hurtfull, and the rather to Hives of ſtraw: and therefore coverings of ſtraw draw them: they will in either at the mouth, or ſhear themſelves an hole: the remedy is good Cats, Rats-bane, and watching.

The cleanly Bee hateth the ſmoak as poyſon; therefore let your bees ſtand nearer your garden, then your Brew-houſe or Kitchen.

They ſay Sparrows and Swallowes are enemies to Bees, but I ſee it not.

More Hives periſh by Winters cold, then by all other hurts: for the bee is tender and nice, and onely lives in warm weather, and dyes in cold: And therefore let my Houſe-wife be perſwaded, that a warm dry houſe before deſcribed, is the chiefeſt help ſhe can make her bees againſt this, and many more miſchiefes. Many uſe againſt cold in winter, to ſtop up their hive cloſe & ſome ſet them in houſes perſwading themſelves, that thereby they relieve their Bees. Firſt toſſing, moving, is hurtfull. Secondly, in houſes, going, knocking, & ſhaking is noyſom. Thirdly, too much heat in an houſe is unnaturall for them : But laſtly, and eſpecially, Bees cannot abide to be ſtopt cloſe up. For at every warme ſeaſon of the Sunne they revive, and living eat, and eating muſt needs purge

Annoyances.

purge abroad : in her houfe the cleanly Bee will not purge her
felf. Judge you what it it for any living creature, not to dif-
burden nature. Being fhut up in calme feafons, lay your ear to
the Hive and you fhall hear them yearn and yell, as fo many hundred prifoners. Therefore impound not your bees, fo profitable
and free a creature.

Let none ftand above three years, elfe the combs will be black
and knotty, your honey will be thin and uncleanly: and if any
caft after three years it is fuch as have fwarmes of old bees kept
alltogether, which is great loffe. Smoaking with Raggs, Rozen,
or brimftone, many ufe: fome ufe drowning in a tub of clean
water, and the water well brew'd, will be good botchet. Draw
out your fpelks immediately with a pair of pinchers, left the
Wood grow foft and fwell, and fo will not be drawn, then muft
you cut your Hive. **Taking of Bees.**

Let no fire come near your honey, for fire foftneth the Waxe
and drofs, and makes them run with the Honey. Fire foftneth
weakeneth, and hindereth Hony for purging. Break your combes
fmall when the dead empty combes are parted from the loaden
Combes into a fieve, born over a great bowl, or veffel with two
ftaves, and fo let it run two or three dayes. The fooner you tun
it up, the better will it purge. Run your fwarme Honey by it
felf, and that fhall be your beft. The elder your Hives are, the
worfe is your honey. **Strayning honey.**

Ufuall Veffels are of Clay, but after wood be fatiated with
Honey (for it will leake at firft: for honey is marvelloufly fear-
ching though thick, & therefore vertuous) I ufe it rather, becaufe
it will not break fo foon with falls, frofts, or otherwife, and greater veffels of clay will hardly laft. **Veffels.**

When you ufe your honey, with a fpoon take off the skin
which it hath put up.

And it is worth the regard, that bees thus ufed, if you have
but forty ftocks, fhall yeeld you more commodity clearely than
forty Acres of Ground.

And thus much may fuffice, to make good Houfewives love
and have good gardens and Bees.

Deo laus.
FINIS.

The

The Contents of the Country Houſe-wifes Garden.

A

A

MOST PROFITABLE
New Treatife, from approved experience of the Art of propagating *Plants*.

By S I M O N H A R VV A R D.

CHAP. I.

The Art of propagating Plants.

THere are foure forts of planting or propagating, as in laying of fhoots or little
branches, whiles they are yet tender, in
fome pit made at their foot, as fhall be
faid hereafter, or upon a little ladder or
basket of earth, tied to the bottome of the
brach, or in boaring a Willow thorow,
and putting the branch of the tree into
the hole, as fhall be fully declared in the
Chapter of Grafting.

There are likewife feafons to propagate in ; but the beft is in   1.
                              M   the

the fpring, and *March*, when the trees are in the Flowre, and do begin to grow lufty. The young planted Siens or little grafts' muft be propagated in the beginning of winter, a foot deep in the earth, and good manure mingled amongft the earth, which you fhall caft forth of the pit wherein you mean to propagate it, to tumble it in upon it againe. In like manner, your fuperfluous Siens, or little plants muft be cut clofe by the earth, when as they grow about fome fmall Impe which we mean to propagate for they will do nothing but rot: For to propagate, you muft dig the earth round about the tree, that fo your roots may be laid in a manner halfe bare. Afterwards draw into length the pit on that fide where you mean to propagate, and according as you perceive that the roots will be beft able to yeeld, and be governed in the fame pit, to ufe them, and that with all gentleneffe, and ftop clofe your Siens, in fuch fort, as that the wreath which is in the place where it is grafted, may be a little lower than the Siens of the new wood growing out of the earth, even fo high as it poffible may be. If the trees that you would propagate be fomewhat thick, and thereby the harder to ply, and fomewhat ftiff to lay in the pit: then you may wet the ftock almoft to the midft, betwixt the root and the wreathing place, fo with gentle handling of it, bow down into the pit the wood which the grafts have put forth, and that in as round a compaffe as you can, keeping you from breaking of it: afterward lay over the cut with gummed wax, or with gravell and fand.

CHAP. 2.
Grafting in the Barke.

GRafting in the barke, is ufed from mid-*Auguft*, to the beginning of Winter, and alfo when the Weftern-wind beginneth to blow, being from the 7 of *February*, unto the 11 of *Iune* But there muft care be had, not to graffe in the barke in any rainy feafon, becaufe it would wafh away the matter of joyning the one and the other together, and fo hinder it.

Grafting in the bud is ufed in the Summer time, from the end of *May*, untill *Auguft*, as being the time, when the trees are ftrong and lufty, and full of fap and leaves. To wit, in a hot Country, countiy from the midlt of *June*, unto the midit of *July*, but in cold Countries to the midſt of *Auguſt*, after ſome ſmall ſhowers of Raine.

If the Summer be ſo exceedingly dry, as that ſome trees doe withold their ſap, you muſt waite the time till it doe returne.

Graft from the full of the moon, untill the end of the old.

You may graft in a cleft, without having regard to Raine, for the ſap will keep it off.

You may graft from mid-*Auguſt*, to the beginning of *November* : Cowes dung with ſtraw doth mightily preſerve the graft.

It is better to graft in the evening than the morning.

The furniture and tooles of a Grafter, are a basket to lay his grafts in, Clay, Gravell, Sand, or ſtrong Earth, to draw over the plants cloven Moſſe, Woollen clothes, barks of VVillow to joyne to the late things and earth before ſpoken ; and to keep them faſt : Oziers to tye againe upon the barke, to keep them firme and faſt, gummed VVax to dreſſe and cover the ends and tops of the grafts newly cut, that ſo the raine and cold may not hurt them, neither yet the ſap riſing from below, be conſtrained to return againe unto the ſhootes. A little Saw or hand-Saw, to ſaw off the ſtock of the plants, a little Knife or Penknife to graffe, and to cut and ſharpen the grafts, that ſo the bark may not pill nor be broken ; which often commeth to paſſe when the graft is full of ſap You ſhall cut the graffe ſo long ; as that it may fill the cliffe of the plant, and therewithall it muſt be left thicker on the bark-ſide, that ſo it may fill up both the cliffe and other inciſions, as any neede is to be made, which muſt be all wayes well ground, well burniſhed without all ruſt. Two wedges, the one broad for thick trees, the other narrow for leſſe and tender trees, both of them of box or ſome other hard and ſmooth wood, or ſteel, or of very hard iron, that ſo they may need leſſe labour in making them ſharpe.

A little hand-bill to ſet the plants at more liberty, by cutting off ſuperfluous boughs, helved of Ivory, box, or braſill.

M 2   CHAP.

CHAP. 3.
Grafting in the Cleft.

THe maner of grafting in a cleft, to wit, the ftock being clov'd, is proper not onely to trees, which are as great as a mans legs or arms, but alfo to greater. It is true that being trees cannot eafily be cloven, in their ftock : that therefore it is expedient to make incifion in fome one of their branches, and not in the main body, as wee fee to be pra&ifed in great Apple-tree?, and great Peare-trees, and as we have already delared heretofore.

To graft in the cleft, you muft make choyce of a graft that is full of fap and juyce, but it muft not be, but till from after *January* untill *March* : And you muft not thus graft in any tree that is already budded, becaufe a great part of the juyce and fap would be already mounted up on high, and rifen to the top, and there difperfed and fcattered hither and thither, into every fprig and twig, and ufe nothing welcome to the graft.

You muft likewife be refolved not to gather your graft the day you graft in, but ten or twelve dayes before : for otherwife if you graft it new gathered it will not be able eafily to incorporate it felf with the body, and ftock, where it fhall be grafted ; becaufe that fome part of it will dry, and by this means will be a hindrance in the ftock to the rifing up of the fap, which it fhould communicate unto the graft, for the making of it to put forth, and whereas this dried part will fall a crumbling, and breaking through his rottenneffe, it will caufe to remaine a concavity, or hollow place in the ftock, which will be an occafion of a like inconvenience to befall the graft. Moreover, the graft being new and tender, might eafily be hurt of the bands, which are of neceffity to be tyed about the Stock, to keep the graft firme and faft. And you muft further fee, that your Plant was not of late removed, but that it have already fully taken root.

7. When you are minded to graft many grafts into one cleft, you muft fee that they be cut in the end all alike.

See that the grafts be of one length, or not much differing, and it is enough, that they have three or foure eylets without the Wrench when the Plant is once fawed, and lopped of all his bran-

branches, if it have many: then you must leave but two at the most before you come to the cleaving of it ; then put to your little Saw, or your knife, or other edged toole that is very sharp, cleave it quite thorow the middest, in gentle and soft sort : First, tying the stock very sure, that so it may not cleave further then is need : and then put to your wedges into the cleft untill such time as you have set in your grafts, and in cleaving of it, hold the knife with the one hand, and the tree with the other, to help to keep it from cleaving too far. Afterwards put in your wedge of Box or brazill, or bone, at the small end ; so that you may the better take it out again, when you have set in your grafts.

If the stock be cloven, or the bark loosed too much from the wood : then cleave it down lower, and set your grafts in and look that their Incision be fit, and very justly answerable to the cleft, and that the two saps, first, of the plant and graft, be right and even set one against the other, and so handsomely fitted, as that there may not be be the least appearance of any cut or cleft For if they doe not thus jump one with anotoer, they will never take one with another, because they cannot work their seeming matter, and as it were cartilaginous glue in convenient sort or manner to the gluing of their joynts together. You must likewise beware, not to make your cleft overthwart the pich, but some-what aside.

The bark of your plant being thicker then that of your graft you must set the graft so much the more outwardly in the cleft, that so the two saps may in any case be joyned, and set right the one with the other, but the rind of the plant must be somewhat more out then that of the grafts or cloven side·

To the end that you may not faile of this work of imping, you must principally take heed, not to over-cleave the stocks of your trees. But before you widen the cleft with your wedges, bind and go about the stock with two or three turnes, and that with an Ozier, close drawne together, underneath the same place, where you would have your cleft to end, that so your stock cleave not too far, which is a very usuall cause of the miscarrying of grafts, in as much as hereby the cleft standeth so wide and open, as that it cannot be shut, and so not grow together againe ; but in the mean time spendeth it self, and breatheth out all his life in
that

10.

that place, which is the cause that the stock & the Graft are both spilt. And this falleth out most often in Plum-trees, and branches of trees. You must be carefull to joyn the rinds of your grafts, and plants, that nothing may continue open, to the end that the wind, moisture of the Clay or Raine running upon the grafted place, do not get in : when the plant cleaveth very streight, there

10. is not any danger nor hardnesse in sloping downe the Graft. If you leave it somewhat uneven or rough in some places, or that the saps both of the one and of the other may the better grow, and be glued together, when your grafts are once well joyned to your plants, draw out your wedges very softly, least you displace them again : you may leave therewith in the cleft some small end of a wedge of green wood, cutting it very close with the head of the Stock Some cast glue into the cleft, some sugar, and some gummed Wax.

11. If the Stock of the Plant, where upon you intend to graft, be not so thick as your graft, you shall graft it after the fashion of a Goat s foot: make a cleft in the stock of the plant, not direct, but byas, and that smooth and eeven, not rough : then apply and make fast thereto the graft with all his bark on, and answering to the bark of the Plant. This being done, cover the place with the fat earth and moss of the Woods tyed together with a strong band: stick a pole of Wood by it to keep it stedfast.

<h3 style="text-align:center">CHAP. 4.</h3>
Grafting like a Scutcheon.

IN grafting after the manner of a Scutcheon, you shall not vary nor differ much from that of the Flute or pipe, save only that the Scutcheon like graft having one eylet, as the other hath yet the wood of the tree whereupon the Scutcheon-like graft is grafted hath not any knob or bud, as the wood whereupon the graft is grafted after the manner of a Pipe.

In Summer when the trees are well replenished with sap, and that their new Siens begin to grow somewhat hard, you
12. shall take a shoot at the end of the chief branches of some noble and reclaimed trees : whereof you would faine have some fruit, and not many of his old store or wood, and from thence raise a good eylet, the taile and all, thereof to make your grafts. But when you choose, take the thickest, and grossest, divide the tail in
the

the midft before you do any thing elfe,cafting away the leaf(if
it be not a pear-plum-tree : for that would have two or three
leaves)without removing any more of the faid taile : afterward
with the point of a fharp knife, cut off the Bark of the faid
fhoot,the pattern of a fhield,of the length of a nail

In which there is onely one eylet higher then the midft together with the refidue of the taile which you left behind:and for
the lifting up of the faid graft in Scutcheon, after that you have
cut the bark of the fhoot round about without cutting of the
wood within, you muft take it gently with your thumbe,and in
putting it away you muft prefs upon the wood from which you
pull it, that fo you may bring the bud and all away together
with the Scutcheon : for if you leave it behind with the wood,
then were the Scutcheon nothing worth You fhall find out if
the Scutcheon be nothing worth, if looking, within when it is
pulled away from the wood of the fame fuit,you find it to have
a hole within,but more manifeftly, if the bud do ftay behind in
the wood,which ought to have been in the Scutcheon.

Thus your Scutcheon being well raifed and taken off,hold
it a little by the tayle betwixt your lips, without wetting of it
even untill you have cut the bark of the tree where you would
graft it, and look that it be cut without any wounding of the
wood within,after the manner of a crutch,but fomewhat longer
then the Scutcheon that you have to fet in it, and in no place
cutting the wood within;after you have made incifion,you muft
open it and make it gape wide on both fides, but in all manner
of gentle handling;& that with a little Sizers of bone, & fepara-
ting the wood and the bark a little within, even fo much as
your Scutcheon is in length and breadth : you muft take heed
that in doing hereof,you do not hurt the bark

This done take your Scutcheon by the end, and your taile
which you have left remaining,and put into your incifion made
in your tree,lifting up foftly your two fides of the incifion with
your faid Sizers of bone, and caufe the faid Scutcheon to joyn,
and lye as clofe as may be,with the wood of the tree, being cut
as aforefaid,in waying a little upon the end of your rinde : fo
cut and let the upper part of your Scutcheon lye clofe unto the
upper end of your incifion,or bark of your faid tree: afterward
bind

13.

14.

15.

binde your Scutcheon about with a band of Hempe. as thick as
a pen of a quill, more or less, according as your tree is small or
great, taking the same Hempe in the midd ft, to the end that
either part of it may performe a like service ; and wreathing
and binding of the said Scutcheon into the incision of a tree; and
it must not be tyed too straight, for that will keep it from taking
the joyning of the one sap to the other being hindred thereby,
and neither the Scutcheon nor yet the Hempe must be moist or
wet : and the more justly to bind them together, begin at the
back side of the tree, right over against the middest of the incision, and from thence come forward to joyne them before, a-
bove the eylet and taile of the Scutcheon crossing your band
of Hempe, so oft as the two ends meet; and from thence return-
ing back againe, come about and tye it likewise underneath the
eylets and thus cast about your b nd still backward and forward
until the whole cleft of the incision be covered above and below
with the said Hempe, the eylet onely excepted, and his taile,

17.
which must not be coverd at all ; his taile will fall away one
part after another, and that shortly after the ingrafting, if so be
the Scutcheon will take. Leave your trees and Scutcheons thus
bound for the space of one month ; and the thicker, a great
deale longer time. Afterward look them over, and if you perceive them to grow together untye them, or at leastwise cut the
Hempe behind them, and leave them uncovered. Cut also
your branch two or three fingers above that, so the impe may
prosper the better : and thus let them remain till after VVinter,
about the month of *March*, and *Aprill*.

18.
If you perceive that the budde of your Scutcheon doe swell
and come forward , then cut off the tree three fi gers or there-
bouts, above the Scutcheon : for if it be cut off too near the
Scutcheon, at such time as it putteth forth his first blossome, it
would be a means greatly to hinder the flowing of it, and cause
also that it should not thrive and prosper so well : after that one
yeer is past, and that the shoote beginneth to be strong , beginning to put forth the second bud and blossome, you must go forward to cut off in byaswise the three fingers in the top of the tree
which you left there, when you cut it in the year going before, as
hath been said.

VVhen

When your fhoote fhall have put forth a great deal of length, you may ftick down there, even hard joyned thereunto, little ftakes, tying them together very gently and eafily ; and thefe fhall ftay your fhoots and prop them up, letting the wind from doing any harm unto them. Thus you may graft white Rofes in red, and red in white. Thus you may graft two or three Scutche-ons: provided that they be all of one fide : for they will not be fet equally together in height, becaufe then they would be all ftarvelings, neither would they be directly one over another; for the lower would ftay the rifing up of the fap of the tree, and fo thofe above fhould confumne in penurie, and undergo the a-forefaid inconvenience. You muft note, that the Scutcheon which is gathered from the Sien of a tree whofe fruit is fowre, muft be cut in fquare forme, and not in the plain fafhion of a Scutcheon. It is ordinary to graffe the fweet Quince tree, baftard Peach-tree, Apricock-tree, Jujube tree, fowre Cherry-tree, fweet Cherry-tree, and Cheftnut-tree, after this fafhion, howbeit they may be grafted in the cleft more eafily, and more profitably ; although divers be of a contrary opinion, as thus : Take the grafts of fweet Quince-tree, and Baftard peach-tree, of the faireft wood, and beft fed that you can find, growing upon the wood of two years old, becaufe the wood is not fo firme and folid as the others ; and you fhall graft them upon fmall Plum-tree ftocks, being of the thickneffe of ones thumbe ; thefe you fhall cut after the manner of a Goats foot : you fhall not goe about to make the cleft of any more fides then one, being about a foot high from the ground; you muft open it with your fmall wedge : and being thus grafted, it will feeme to you that it is open but of one fide ; afterward you fhall wrap it up with a little Moffe, putting thereto fome gummed Wax, or Claie, and bind it up with Oziers to keep it furer, becaufe the ftock is not ftrong e-nough it felf to hold it. and you fhall furnifh it every manner of way as others are dealt withall; this is moft profitable.

The time of Grafting.

All Months are good to graft in, (the Month of *October* and *November* onely excepted) But commonly, graft at that time of

N   the

the winter, when the fap beginneth to arife.

In a cold Countrie graft later, in a warme Country earlier.

The beft time generally is from the firft of *February,* untill the firft of *May.*

The grafts muft alwaies be gathered, in the old of the Moone.

For grafts choofe fhoots of a yeare old, or at the furthermoft two years old.

If you muft carry grafts far, prick them into a Turnep newly gathered or lay earth about the ends.

If you Set ftones of Plummes, Almonds, Nuts, or Peaches: Firft let them lye a little in the Sun, and then fteep them in Milk or Water three or four dayes, before you put them into the earth.

Drie the Kernels of Pippins, and fow them in the end of *November.*

The ftone of a Plum-tree muft be Set a foot deep, in *November* or *February.*

The Date-ftone muft be Set the great end downwards, two cubits deep in the earth, in a place enriched with dung.

The Peach-ftone would be Set prefently after the Fruit is eaten, fome quantity of the flefh of the Peach remaining about the ftone.

If you would have it to be excellent, graft it afterward upon an Almond tree.

The little Siens of Cherry-trees, grown thick with haire, rots and thofe alfo which doe grow up from the roots of the great Cherry-trees, being removed, do grow better and fooner then they which come of ftones: but they muft be removed and planted while they are but two or three years old, the branches muft be lopped.

The

A very profitable Invention, for the speedy
planting of an Orchard of
Fruit-Trees.

ABout the end (or rather the middle) of *June* the sap being then in the boughes or tops of the Trees, let some one of discretion goe up into the boughes of the Tree intended, and with a keen-knife cut the bark of some smooth bough so chosen round about the same, quite through the same bark, to the very bare wood, in two places (toward the but of the bough) a full hand breadth the one from the other, & take off the bark clean clearly from the said bough, and cast it away, and wipe the sap off that bared place; Then take some of the stiffest clay you can have, and wrap it hard, round about the said bared place (that it may stop the sap when it descendeth;) bind on this clay with fallow slings or the like, very hard; let this clay be two inches thick at least. Then prepare a certaine quantity of good ranke mould, tempered with short muck and misken water, and make mortar thereof, and wrap a good quantity of it as big as a foot ball, upon the firm barke remaining close above the said clay, that it may touch the same; put mosse upon it, & as before, bind it well, and so let it continue growing upon the same Tree till *February*. Then with a fine saw carefully take off the said bough close below the clay, not perishing the upper mortar; and set that bough, with the clay and mortar on it, in some good ground, and there let it remain to grow; for the sap it cannot passe downward for the clay but stayeth in the upper mortar, and breeds roots, and possibly (God willing) may bear fruit the next Summer following. Thus you may order many such boughes as aforesaid, and quickly plant an Orchard of bearing Trees. If the bough be as big as the small of ones leg, it is so much the better: *probatum est.*

N 2   The

The Contents of the Art of
Propagating Plants.

THE
HUSBAND MANS
FRUITFUL ORCHARD.

For the true ordering of all forts of
Fruits in their due feafons : and how double
increafe cometh by care in gathering yeer after
year: as alfo the beft way of carriage by land
or by water, with their prefervation
for longeft continuance.

F all ftone Fruit, Cherries are the firft to be
gathered : of which though we reckon foure
forts; *Englifh*, *Flemmifh*, *Gafcoigne*, and *Black*,
yet are they reduced to two, the early, and the
ordinary ; the early are thofe whofe grafts
came firft from *France* and *Flanders*, and are
now ripe with us in *May*: the ordinary is our
own naturall Cherry, and is not ripe before *June* : they muft
be carefully kept from Birds, either with nets, noife, or other
induftry.

They

Gathering of Cherries,

They are not all ripe at once, nor may be gathered at once, therefore with a light Ladder made to stand of it self without hurting the boughes, mount to the tree, and with a gathering hook, gather those which be full ripe, and put them into your Cherry-pot, or Kybzey hanging by your side, or upon any bough you please, & be sure to break no stalk, but that the cherry hangs byland pull them gently, lay them down tenderly, and handle them as little as you can.

To carry Cherries.

For the conveyance or portage of Cherries, they are best to be carried in broad Baskets like sives, with smooth yeelding bottomes, only two broad laths going along the bottome : and if you do transport them by ship, or boat, let not the sives be filled to the top, left setting one upon another, you bruise and hurt the Cherries : if you carry by horseback, then panniers well lined with Fearne, and packt full and close is the best and safest way.

Other stone-fruit.

Now for the gathering of all other stone fruit, as Nectarines, Apricocks, Peaches, Peare-plummes, Damsons, Bullas, and such like although in their severall kinds, they seem not to be ripe at once on one tree : yet when any is ready to drop from the tree, though the other seem hard, yet they may also be gathered, for they have received the full substance the tree can give them ; and therefore the day being faire, and the dew drawn away ; set up your Ladder, and as you gathered your Cherries so gather them: onely in the bottomes of your large sives, where you part them, you shall lay Nettles, and likewise in the top, for that will ripen those that are most unready.

Gathering of Peares.

In gathering of Peares are three things observed: to gather for expence, for transportation, or to sell to the Apothecary. If for expence, and your own use, then gather them as soon as they change, and are as it were half ripe, and no more but those which are changed, letting the rest hang till they change also : for thus they will ripen kindly, & not rot so soon, as if they were full ripe at the gathering. But if your Peares be to be transporter far either by Land or Water, then pull one from the Tree, and cut it in the middest, and if you find it hollow about the coare, and the kernell a large space to lye in, although no Peare be

ready to drop from the Tree yet then they may be gathered,
and then laying them on a heap one upon another, as of
neceffity they muft be for tranfportation, theywill ripen of
themfelves and eat kindly : but gathered before, they will
wither,fhrinke and eate rough , lofing not onely their taft, but
beauty.

Now for the manner of gathering; albeit fome clime into the Gathering of
trees by the boughes,and fome by Ladder, yet both is amiffe ; the Apples.
beft way is with the Ladder before fpoken of,which ftandeth of it
felfe,with a basket & a line,which being full,you muft gently let
down,and keeping the ftring ftill in your hand, being emptied,
draw it up againe,and fo finifh your labour, without troubling
your felf,or hurting the Tree.

Now touching the gathering of Apples,it is to be done according to the ripening of the fruit ; your Summer Apples firft,
and the Winter after.

For Summer fruit, when it is ripe, fome will drop from the
Tree,and Birds will be picking at them : But if you cut out one
of the greeneft,and find it as was fhew'd you before of the peare :
then you may gather them, and in the houfe they will come to
their ripneffe and perfection. For your Winter fruit, you fhall
know the ripenefs by the obfervation before fhewed;but it muft
be gathered in a faire,Sunnie, and dry day, in the waine of the
Moone, and no Wind in the Eaft, alfo after the dew is gone
away;for the leaft wet or moyfture will make them fubject to rot
and mildew ; alfo you muft have an apron to gather in, and to
empty into the great basket, and a hook to draw the boughes
unto you,which you cannot reach with your hands at eafe : the
apron is to be an Ell every way, loopt up to your girdle, fo
as it may ferve for either hand without any trouble : and
when it is full, unloofe one of your loopes, and empty it
gently into the great basket, for in throwing them downe
roughly, their owne ftalkes may prick them , and thofe
which are prick, will ever rot. Againe, you muft gather your fruit cleane without leaves or brunts , becaufe the
one hurts the tree, for every brunt would be a ftalk for fruit
to grow upon:the other,hurts the fruit by bruifing, and pricking
it,as it is laid together, and there is nothing fooner rotteth
fruit,

fruit, then the green and and withered leaves lying among them ;
neither muſt you gather them without any ſtalke at all : for ſuch
fruit will begin to rot where the ſtalk ſtood.

For ſuch fruit as falleth from the trees, and are not gathered,
they muſt not be layd with the gathered fruit : and of fallings
there are two ſorts ; one that falls through ripeneſſe, and they
are beſt, and may be kept to bake or roaſt : the other windfals,
falling before they are ripe; & they muſt be ſpent as they are gathered or elſe they will wither and come to nothing ; and therefore
it is not good by any means to beat downe fruit with Poles,
or to carry them in carts looſe and jogging, or in ſacks where
they may be bruiſed.

When your fruit is gathered, you ſhall lay them in deep Baskets of Wicker, which ſhall contain four or ſix buſhels, and ſo
between two men, carry them to your Apple Loft ; and in
ſhooting or laying them downe, be very carefull that it
be done with all gentleneſſe, and leaſure, laying every ſort of
fruit ſeverally by it ſelf: but if there be want of roome, having ſo
many ſorts that you cannot lay them ſeverally, then ſome ſuch
fruit as is neareſt in taſt and colour, and of Winter fruit, ſuch
as will taſt alike, may, if need require, be laid together, and in
time you may ſeperate them, as ſhall be ſhewed hereafter. But
if your fruit be gathered far from your Apple-Loft, then muſt
the bottomes of your Baſkets be lined with green Ferne, and
draw the ſtubborne ends of the ſame through the Basket, that
none but the ſoft leaf may touch the fruit, and likewiſe cover
the tops of the Baſkets with Fearne alſo, and draw ſmall
cord over it, that the Ferne may not fall away, nor the fruit
ſcatter out, or jogge up and downe : and thus you may carry
fruit by Land or by Water, by Boat, or Cart, as farre as
you pleaſe : and the Ferne doth not onely keep them from
bruiſing, but alſo ripens them, eſpecially Peares. When
your fruit is brought to your Apple Loft, or ſtore-houſe,
if you find them not ripened enough, then lay them in thicker
heaps upon Ferne, and cover them with Ferne alſo : and when
they are neer ripe, then uncover them and make the heaps thin-
ner, ſo as the ayr may paſſe through them : and if you will not
haſten the ripening of them, then lay them on the boards without

out any Fearne at all. Now for Winter, or long lasting Peares, they may be packt either in Ferne or Straw, and carried whither you please; and being come to the journeys end must be laid upon sweet straw; but beware the roome be not too warme, nor windy; and too coole, for both are hurtfull : but in a temperate place, where they may have ayre, but not too much.

Wardens are to be gathered, carried, packt, and laid as Winter Of wardens. Peares are.

Medlers are to be gathered about *Michaelmas*, after a frost Of Medlers. hath toucht them; at which time they are in their full growth, and will then be dropping from the tree, but never ripe upon the tree. When they are gathered, they must be laid in a basket, sieve, barrell, or any such cask, and wrapt about with woollen cloths, under, over, and on all sides, and also some weight laid upon them, with a board between : for except they be brought into a heat, they will never ripen kindly, or taft well.

Now when they have laine till you thinke some of them be ripe, the ripest, still as they ripen, must be taken from the rest; therefore powre them out into another sieve or basket leasurely, that so you may well find them that be ripest, letting the hard ones fall into the other basket, and those which be ripe laid aside: the other that be halfe ripe sever also into a third sieve or basket: for if the ripe and halfe ripe be kept together, the one will be mouldy, before the other be ripe : And thus doe till all be throughly ripe.

Quinces should not be laid with other fruit, for the sent is Of Quinces. offensive both to other fruit, and to those that keep the fruit or come amongst them: therefore lay them by themselves upon sweet straw, where they may have ayre enough : they must be packt like Medlers, and gathered with Medlers.

Apples must be packt in Wheat or Rye-straw, and in maunds To pack or baskets lyned with the same, and being gently handled, will Apples. ripen with such packing and lying together. If several sorts of apples be packt in one maund or basket, then betweene every sort lay sweet straw of a pretty thicknesse·

Apples must not bee powred out, but with care and lea- Emptying and sure : first, the straw pickt cleane from them, and then gently laying Apples

O   take

take out every feverall fort, and place them by themfelves : but if for want of room you mixe the forts together, then lay thofe together that are of equal lafting : but if they have all one taft, then they need no feparation. Apples that are not of like colours fhould not be laid together, and if any fuch be mingled, let it be amended, and thofe which are firft ripe, let them be firft fpent, and to that end, lay thofe apples together; that are of one time of ripening : and thus you muft ufe Pippins alfo, yet will they indure bruifes better then any other fruit, and whilft they are green will heale one another.

Difference in fruit. Pippins though they grow of one tree, and in one ground, yet fome will laft better then other fome, and fome will be bigger then others of the fame kind, according as they have more or leffe of the Sun, or more or leffe of the droppings of the trees or upper branches : therefore let every one make moft of that fruit which is faireft, and longeft lafting. Againe, the largeneffe and goodneffe of fruit confifts in the age of the tree : for as the tree increafeth, fo the fruit increafeth in bigneffe, beauty, taft, and firmneffe: and otherwife as it decreafeth.

Tranfporting fruit by water. If you be to tranfport your fruit far by water, then provide fome dry hogges-heads or barrells and packe in your apples, one by one, with your hand, that no empty place may be left, to occafion fogging; and you muft line your veffel at both ends with fine fweet ftraw; but not the fides, to avoid heat : and you muft bore a dozen holes at either end, to receive ayre fo much the better; and by no meanes let them take wet. Some ufe, that tranfport beyond feas, to fhut the fruit under hatches upon ftraw: but it is not fo good, if caske may be gotten.

When not to tranfport fruit It is not good to tranfport fruit in *March*, when the wind blowes bitterly, nor in frofty weather, neither in the extreame heat of Summer:

To convey fmall ftore of fruit. If the quantity be fmall you would carry, then you may carry them in doffers or Panniers, provided they may be ever filled clofe; and that Cherries and Peares be lined with green Fearne, and Apples with fweet ftraw; and that, but at the bottomes and tops, not on the fides.

Roomes for fruit. Winter fruit muft lye neither too hot, nor too cold, too clofe nor too open : for all are offenfive. A low roome or Cellar

th

that is fweet, and either boarded or paved, and not too clofe, is good, from *Chriftmas* till *March*: and roomes that are fieled over head, and from the ground, are good from *March* till *May*, then the Cellar againe, from *May* till *Michaolmas*. The apple-loft would be fieled or boarded, which if it want, take the longeft Rye-ftraw, and raife it againft the walls, to make a fence as high as the fruit lyeth ; and let it be no thicker then to keep the fruit from the wall, which being moyft, may doe hurt, or if not moift, then the duft is offenfive.

Sorting of fruit.

There are fome fruit which will laft but untill *Allhallontide*: they muft be laid by themfelves; then thofe which will laft till *Chriftmas*, by themfelves; then thofe which will laft till it be *Candlemas*, by themfelves ; thofe that will laft till *Shrovetide*, by themfelves ; and Pippins , Apple-Johns, Peare-maines , and Winter Ruffettings , which will laft all the yeer, by them-felves.

Now if you fpy any rotten fruit in your heapes, pick them out, and with a Tray for the purpofe, fee you turne the heapes over, and leave not a tainted Apple in them, dividing the hardeft by themfelves, and the broken skinned by themfelves to be firft fpent, and the rotten ones to be caft away; and ever as you turne them, and pick them, under-lay them with frefh ftraw: thus fhall you keep them for your ufe , which otherwife would rot fud-denly.

Time of ftir-ring fruit.

Pippins, John-Apples, Peare maines, and fuch like long lafting fruit, need not to be turned till the week before *Chriftmas*, un-leffe they be mixt with other of riper kind, or that the fallings be alfo with them, or much of the firft ftraw left amongft them: the next time of turning is at *Shrove-tide*, and after that once a month till *Whitfon-tide*; and after that, once a fortnight : and ever in the turning lay your heapes lower and lower, and your ftraw very thinne: provided you doe none of this labour in any great froft, except it be in a clofe Celler. At every thaw, all fruit is moyft, and then they muft not be touched : neither in rainy weather, for then they will be danke alfo ; and therefore at fuch feafons it is good to fet open your windowes and doores , that the ayre may have free paffage to dry them, as at nine of the clock in the forenoon in Winter; and at fixe in the fore-noone,

O 2   and

and at eight at night in Summer;onely in *March*,open not your windowes at all.

All lasting fruit,after the midst of *May*, begin to wither, because then they wax dry,and the moisture gone,which made them looke plumpe,they must needes wither, and be small; and nature decaying,they must needs rot And thus much touching the ordering of fruits.

FINIS.